Moody Bible Institute:

God's Power in Action

Moody Bible Institute:

God's Power in Action

By

DOROTHY MARTIN

MOODY PRESS

CHICAGO

Moody Press, a ministry of the Moody Bible Institute, is
designed for education, evangelization, and edification.
If we may assist you in knowing more about Christ and
the Christian life, please write us without obligation:
Moody Press, c/o MLM, Chicago, Illinois 60610

Library of Congress Cataloging in Publication Data

Martin, Dorothy McKay, 1921-
    Moody Bible Institute: God's power in action.
    1. Moody Bible Institute of Chicago. I. Title.
BV4070.M76M37   269'.2'06277311   76-49492
ISBN 0-8024-5518-2

Printed in the United States of America

Contents

MOODY STARED OUT at the ravaged city. Everywhere, blackened ruins leaned grotesquely over people searching for bits of treasured memories.

But his stocky figure carried an even heavier burden than the loss of his own home and possessions and treasures. It was the memory of last Sunday's evening service.

He remembered how the congregation had listened intently through the uncomfortable October heat. He had finished his message while firebells clanged in the distant night. He had leaned forward earnestly. "In these troubled times—in your troubled lives, what will you do with Jesus which is called Christ?"

He had looked out at the faces, his own heart beating with the seriousness of the question. "Think about Him this week, and come next Sunday to make your decision."

The congregation had gone out to the smell of smoke, heavy in the night air. Hours later many of them were gone; lost in the blazing fury of the fire.

Mr. Moody bowed in prayer, grief stricken. Never again, *never again* would he send anyone away without giving a direct, urgent invitation to accept Christ.

1

D. L. Moody: Crystallizing a Vision

HISTORY TREMBLED in the wings those fateful days of the 1850s while war waited its entrance to center stage. The drama taking place was deadly. Conflict in politics and economics exploded the country into the terrible Civil War.

Two paradoxical events marked 1857. One, a panic which crippled people economically; the other, a spiritual revival which swept over the country. But neither event stopped the inexorable march to war. It was more than a war between states, for it set brother against brother, destroyed homes, devastated property, and wasted lives.

When the guns finally fell silent, the country knew another fearful loss. Crowds stood along streets in silent tears as the funeral cortege carried President Abraham Lincoln home for burial.

But the war's end brought economic development which finally overcame bitterness and dissension. A drastic change remolded life in the United States as its cities expanded enormously because of increased immigration and the dramatic Industrial Revolution.

The years from the Civil War to the end of the century are popularly called the Gilded Age, Mark Twain's term of derision about the years of Grant's presidency. But the expression also pictures the rest of the century when an outward sheen of prosperity laid a thin veneer over the raw and ugly.

The raw and ugly showed in the gaps between people. A small group of the very rich clustered at the top. These were men who came to cities like Chicago with empty pockets, and in a few short years by ambition, hard work, and sometimes clever scheming, had bulging vaults. Next came plenty of solid "common people," to use Lincoln's phrase. But below them lay the thick layer of immigrants who came to America expecting golden streets, but found mud. The times seemed out of joint, indeed, to the man working twelve or fourteen hours a day for fifty cents—if he was lucky enough to find a job at all.

The post-Civil War era erupted with problems because of the almost overnight growth of cities which packed people tightly in unheated wooden boxes. The Ku Klux Klan terrorized Blacks, and street-corner saloons took decency from people. Rampant crime, and corruption in city governments and the police force made the man on the street cynical.

But winds of reform also blew. Help came from the Salvation Army, the YMCA, churches, and settlement houses. The most famous of these was Jane Addams' Hull House in Chicago which gave hope to families in desperate conditions. Along with these efforts grew demands for prison reform, for women's rights, for better education. Temperance was hotly debated and the WCTU and the Anti-Saloon League demanded action.

The Social Gospel sprang from this confused background. Its message was the here-and-now effect of the Gospel rather than its eternal redeeming work. Followers talked about the Christianizing of society instead of the salvation of the individual. American religion stood on shaky ground in these years as even ministers and theologians questioned the relevance of Christianity to life's daily problems.

Even more threatening, the shock of Charles Darwin's ideas reverberated across the nation. Those who swallowed them were glad to laugh off the narrow Bible account of creation. Those who believed the Bible were filled with dismay, not knowing what to answer. As if evolution were not enough to unsettle traditional ideas, Christian Science came with its denial of sin and evil; Ralph Waldo Emerson, a respected voice, talked of transcendentalism; New Thought teaching used the word *God* to mean a vague spirit of Love and Joy, but definitely not the personal God of Scripture.

Of course these years were not all darkness and gloom. Many good things happened. Tremendous life-saving medical discoveries gradually wiped out some of the ignorance and superstition. The telephone, the phonograph, electric lights— it seemed something new came every day to make life easier.

So knowledge and ignorance, prosperity and poverty, reform and corruption grew together in the years of the Gilded Age like the wheat and tares in the biblical parable.

Both the good and the evil in the nation focused in Chicago. From its start as a few log cabins clustered in a swampy spot along the Chicago River, it mushroomed to become the leading city of the Midwest. Its motto, "I Will," characterized its citizens' vitality. They needed energy to cope with the gales that blew off restless Lake Michigan, the city's eastern boundary. The lake helped make the only reliable thing about Chicago—its unpredictable weather.

Chicago hosted the stormy convention that nominated Abraham Lincoln to be president, wept with the rest of the country at his death, and dedicated Lincoln Park in his memory. With the end of the Civil War, the city's location guaranteed its growth and prosperity.

Evil flourished in many ways in the crowded city. In the mid-sixties 2,000 saloons and gambling houses took bread, shoes, and decency from families.

And Chicago was a wooden city. The summer of 1871 was unusually dry with hot, high winds blistering rich and poor alike. On Sunday, October 8, the fire, which rumor blamed on Mrs. O'Leary's cow, flamed in the wooden houses set in dense rows one upon another. It was like "setting fire to a box of matches," remembers one who lived through it. Walls of flame raced along the streets with a deafening roar. The fire was so intense it blazed with a minimum of smoke, and people saw only red tongues of flame wrapping around other people and buildings. It consumed tenements and mansions, shoddy restaurants and expensive stores, rags and Persian rugs. Those who survived shuddered at memories of the tremendous roar and crackle of flames, the screams of animals and people, the thundering crash of falling buildings, the acts of mercy, and the appalling cruelties. The survivors lifted grateful faces to the cold rain that mercifully began to fall Monday night and gradually put out the final remnants of flame.

Chicago rose from this devastation into a period of intense growth. From 1871 to 1890 it became the meat packing center of the nation; the grain center of the world; a lumber center; the hub of railroads, banking, investments, and industry. In 1877 the first telephones came to Chicago. Moody and Sankey campaign hymns were among the most popular songs used to demonstrate the new invention.

The city grew vertically as skyscrapers pushed toward the clouds, and horizontally as a well-planned transit system spread west and north and south.

All this activity brought noise—horses' hoofs clattered on the streets, people rushed and shouted, trains screeched. Industry belched coal smoke into the air to blacken buildings and clothes and lungs. The stench from the Chicago River and the stockyards was unbearable at times, and epidemics of malaria, typhoid, and cholera plagued Chicagoans.

Some downtown buildings slowly sank into the mud streets. A sign which one sarcastic humorist posted said, "No bottom here. Shortest route to China." It was no joke to those who lost shoes in the sucking mud.

But the city government boldly tackled these problems. It controlled the pollution of air and water. It jacked up buildings and piled fill several feet deep to raise streets. And it did

more. With the help of the "merchant princes"—Field, Mc-
Cormick, Pullman, Armour, who could give a casual pledge
of ten million or so with a few pen strokes—the Chicago Symphony Orchestra, the Art Institute, and the public library
made the rest of America know that Chicago was a place of
culture.

But clean streets and safe drinking water and museums still
left the great mass in desperate conditions. The glittering
elegance of mansions on Michigan Avenue contrasted starkly
with the "frame jungles" in which much of the city's population lived. The tenement buildings where a whole family
lived and died in one room—"a room where the sun never
enters"— defied belief.

Many immigrants, cultured, refined, educated, were forced
into the slums by economic and cultural barriers. Even language was a barrier to understanding, as it has been since the
Tower of Babel. Immigrants naturally clustered with those
they understood. One woman who came from Poland as a
girl of sixteen lived in her ethnic neighborhood, read papers
in her language, shopped at neighborhood Polish stores.
Though she lived to her nineties, she knew not a word of
English.

Little attempt was made to Americanize immigrants. With
jobs scarce, they met bitter opposition when they took even
the least desirable and lowest-paying work.

Labor unrest seethed in Chicago in the last fourth of the
century. A ball by one of Chicago's richest families cost
$75,000 for the evening. When? In 1886, the year labor's
anger at low wages boiled over in the Haymarket Riot. Depression was worse in the icy winds of winter, and people
starved in spite of soup kitchens set up on vacant lots. The
winter of 1894 was a black one, with babies left on the streets
in hope that someone would take pity on them. Those fortu-
nate enough to be going to work stumbled over the stiff figures
of others who spent the night huddled in doorways.

The moral climate of Chicago festered along with the slum conditions. Crime and vice flourished, while the city government looked the other way and held out a hand for a payoff. Chicago's reputation as a wild town was a magnet attracting lawbreakers. The city was a swirling center of desperate need and dynamic opportunity.

Into the need and the opportunity stepped Dwight L. Moody, a man whose message spoke of redemption for the human heart.

Born in Northfield, Massachusetts, in 1837, Moody grew through his widowed mother's struggle to keep her large family together. The story of his life is familiar. He had only a few years of formal education, but that really was not very important then. Many successful men had spent little time in a school room.

Moody loved fun and in his teenage years was restless at the small-town narrowness of his life. When he was seventeen he left home for Boston and got work in an uncle's shoe store on the condition that he attend church regularly. He did— and accepted Christ as his Saviour through the personal touch of his Sunday school teacher, Edward Kimball. Though he had attended church as a child, Moody knew nothing about the Bible at the time he was saved.

The salvation experience was genuine and changed the direction of his life. But he was still restless and found Boston too confining. He needed a wider door of opportunity for the fortune he planned to build. Exciting, aggressive Chicago was the place to go, and he arrived in September 1856 about the time the revival reached the city.

When he came to Chicago, he stepped through the doorway to adventure for himself and for thousands whose lives he later touched. He immediately did what was usual for the times. He rented pews in one of the churches and invited other young men he met in business to fill the rows with him.

Moody regularly attended the YMCA noon prayer meetings, but he didn't just sit; that was not his nature. Instead, he stood outside the building, urging those hurrying by to stop for prayer.

Moody quickly found employment, again in a shoe store, and again he did not just wait for browsing customers to come in. He went out into the streets after them. He did the same in following another consuming interest—reaching children for Sunday school.

Soon after coming to Chicago, he discovered a Sunday afternoon mission school on the corner of Chicago and Wells and offered to teach a class. Because the school had more than enough teachers, he was told he could teach if he found his own pupils. The next Sunday he brought in eighteen ragged children from the nearby slum area. They were in desperate need of clothes, food, manners, and Christ. So began Moody's lifelong concern for reform and regeneration.

He next started his own mission Sunday school in a public hall over one of Chicago's large city markets north of the Chicago River. Again, what he touched, grew. Who could resist the warm personality of the man who came looking for *you,* sometimes riding a pony, his "missionary horse," and brought you clothes when you had nothing to wear and food if the table was bare. Conscious of his lack of training to teach, Moody did the recruiting, the job he excelled in. He recruited both pupils and helpers, and one of his most enthusiastic supporters was the wealthy merchant John V. Farwell.

Then in June 1860, something happened to Moody. His values took a dramatic turn, and he threw away his desire to make a personal fortune. From then on, his commitment to Christ was complete; illustrated by an anecdote told of him. When Mr. Moody asked a passerby if he was a Christian, the man snapped, "That's none of your business." Moody answered, "That is my business," and the man replied, "Then you must be Mr. Moody."

Reaching people for Christ was his passion and his business for the rest of his life.

When he married young Emma Revell in 1862, the Lord gave him a partner who was completely in sympathy with his purpose and was his quiet but ardent supporter. Though Moody's preaching campaigns frequently took him far from home, he wrote tender, loving letters to his wife and children. He was so glad to get home from these trips that when he came in sight of his house, he ran to meet his family. His wife was to him the "divinely appointed balance wheel of his existence," and smoothed off many of his rough edges.

The desperate needs of soldiers and prisoners during the Civil War led Moody to volunteer his services to the United States Christian Commission. The ten thousand Confederate soldiers barricaded in Chicago's Camp Douglas were not enemies in Moody's eyes, but men needing God's redeeming grace and comfort. These war experiences helped make him known throughout the country, though this was of little importance to him. Many of the soldiers he helped hovered near death as he spoke to them of Christ. This made vivid to him the urgent need of giving the gospel simply and clearly— and briefly.

Moody's creative energy found outlet in many ways. He vigorously supported the struggling YMCA and was president of the Chicago Association in 1866, traveling extensively. The Sunday school movement benefited from the overflow of his enthusiasm. Remembering his own ignorance, he pushed this movement that would teach the Bible to children and adults. As a result he was a popular speaker at Sunday school conventions across the country.

But his heaviest burden was the salvation of those in the slums as he had seen them in the Chicago and Wells Street mission school. He had gone into the squalid rooms and seen the wretchedness with his own eyes. He heard the icy Chicago winds whistle through broken windows, sat on the rickety furniture, saw the rats and cockroaches, and tasted the rancid food. Some reformers talked about the "masses"; Moody saw people—ragged children, thin mothers, overworked fathers. Many times a poor family answered a thundering knock on the door to find Mr. Moody with a basket of food or coal, or with clothes draped over his arm. People's desperate physical needs could easily have overshadowed their spiritual vacuum. But always Moody's relief of hunger and cold came wrapped in the gospel message of eternal satisfaction through Jesus Christ.

His imagination worked constantly, seeking ways to reach people for Christ. He bought a lot at the corner of Illinois and Wells Streets and built the Illinois Street Church which seated 1,500 and was always crowded. This building and Moody's home were destroyed in the Chicago fire, along with the hundreds of other buildings.

Moody plunged immediately into raising money to help the refugees roaming the streets. He also raised money to build a new church, once again balancing the material and the spiritual. During these months his family lived with relatives while he slept in the Northside Tabernacle. Moody moved his family to Northfield soon after the fire, wanting for them the quiet of what once had seemed to him too slow. But he never lost touch with Chicago, and the excitement and opportunity of the city drew him back repeatedly. He saw it as a city of culture and wealth and piety, but also as a city of ignorance and poverty and crime. His imprint remains forever in Chicago in the Moody Bible Institute and the Moody Memorial Church.

But buildings were not the final measure of the man. More important foundations were laid which became living buildings: the people who were saved in Moody's preaching campaigns. Wherever he went, his strategy was to reach the cities. He struck fire in the poor and ignorant as well as in the rich and educated.

And he reached students. On his great campaign in Great Britain, a meeting at Cambridge University began in derision as students shouted their scorn for this unlearned, rotund American who had the gall to speak to them in his American twang and his abrupt, slurred speech. But the meeting ended with many confessing sin and accepting Christ.

Wilfred Grenfell, a medical student in London's worst slums, listened to Moody out of curiosity at a tent meeting. Later Grenfell accepted Christ from the witness of C. T. Studd and became the famous missionary to Labrador. And who was Studd? A second-generation Moody convert. His father was saved in a Moody meeting and witnessed to his son, who later went to China to serve Christ.

Those outside the church often picture an evangelist as a pulpit-pounding, self-serving shouter. Mr. Moody was not that kind of evangelist. Though he spoke with great earnestness and intensity and was sometimes abrupt, he preached with no outward show or emotional appeal except his own warmth. His simple message of God's love for the sinner moved people to respond.

His success in Great Britain from 1873 to 1875 brought Moody world attention. The poorly educated, common man moved from the narrow confines of Northfield to Boston; from there he went to Chicago and an exciting, growing vision; from Chicago he went out to the world, and always with the simple but dynamic message of God's love.

Moody, this man with only a few grades of school, left his most enduring monument in education. He knew God, he believed the Bible, and he was eager to learn from those who were trained. Most of all, he wanted to teach others.

Mr. Moody first founded two schools: one in Northfield, Massachusetts, for girls, and the Mount Hermon School for boys. Then an exciting idea caught fire in Chicago; not a raging, destructive fire, but one that burned in cleansing power. It became the Moody Bible Institute, established in 1886.

The idea came from conversations Moody had with Miss Emma Dryer soon after the Chicago fire. She was a teacher; an intense, devoted woman, burdened for women's needs in an age when women's rights were ignored. The desperate conditions of families after the great fire impressed her with the responsibility Christians should assume: to give people both physical and spiritual aid. Backed by Mrs. Cyrus H. McCormick and other wealthy women, she went into homes with food and Bibles. Moody's imagination was triggered by her Bible classes, and he urged her to start training other women to do this kind of work. But Miss Dryer insisted he was the one to do this kind of job, and that men as well as women should learn to be city evangelists.

Moody had no inclination for a project that would consume time he did not have and energy he needed for other work. And he did not want to start a training program that would seem to compete with seminaries. So he encouraged Miss Dryer to continue her Bible classes and promised to raise money for her work from his wealthy friends.

But these Bible classes were not sufficient—they did not reach enough people or give enough training. Christians began to pray for a more permanent organization. In January 1886, speaking to a large noon crowd in Farwell Hall, Moody talked about the need for a coeducational school to train workers to reach the masses. (Note the year—1886, the year of intense business-labor confrontation, the year of the Haymarket Riot.)

"Either these people are to be evangelized, or the leaven of communism and infidelity will assume such enormous proportions that it will break out in a reign of terror such as this country has never known," Moody warned.

This did not mean he was blind to the rich and powerful who needed salvation. But he was particularly concerned for the seething poor who had nowhere to go in their misery, and so in desperation might follow any leader.

A Chicago newspaper quoted the speech as he spelled out his ideas.

> I tell you . . . what I have on my heart. I would like to see $250,000 raised at once; $250,000 for Chicago is not anything. . . . Then take men that have the gifts and train them for this work of reaching the people.
>
> But you will say: "Where are you going to find them?" I will tell you. God never had a work but what he had men to do it. I believe we have got to have gap-men—men to stand between the laity and the ministers; men who are trained to do city mission work. . . . We need the men that have the most character to go into the shops and meet these hardhearted infidels and skeptics. They have got to know the people and what we want is men that know that, and go right into the shop and talk to men. Never mind the Greek and Hebrew, give them plain English and good Scripture. It is the sword of the Lord that cuts deep.[1]

The money Moody asked for came in quickly to begin this training school for city evangelization. The school received its charter in February 1887, as the Chicago Evangelization Society, for Moody resisted any attempt to have it named for him. For the next several years the Society reached out to Chicago. Two- or three-week training sessions, called institutes, to train people in the Bible and witnessing were held each May throughout the city. These training sessions were brief but intensive. It was a "this is what and how you do it; now, go and do it" course of study. And what better place for a school than Chicago? A training ground lay just outside its doors!

It was not all smooth sailing. Not everyone who promised money gave, and there was cause for hesitation. Moody's frequently impetuous moves made some businessmen uneasy, wanting to put brakes on the whole project. When asked

about definite plans for the new venture, Moody's characteristic answer was, "I intend to keep the school going, red-hot,
all the time." But the question was how he would do it when
he was away from the city much of the time. Who would
actually run the place?

Those who knew him were aware that organization was not
his gift. Establishing, energizing, motivating, inspiring, yes.
But more was needed if an established school was to attract
students and be recognized as a place of value.

And not everyone who promised to help proved helpful.
Ill will and dissension flared among the strong personalities.
Miss Dryer, Mr. Moody, and others involved were demanding,
and at times autocratic in their actions and words. Inevitably
rifts came—as they had with Paul and Barnabas—and Miss
Dryer eventually stepped out of the picture. Mr. Moody was
a leader, an idea man, a forceful, driving personality, impatient with others not as visionary as he. But along with
these traits was a compensating grace; he was willing to apol-
ogize when he had wronged or unjustly criticized someone.

With all this a giant step came in 1889. Moody came to
teach in the training institute sessions held in the Chicago
Avenue Church during April and May. Interest and enthusiasm were so great that as the summer wore on everyone involved began to see the need for a permanent building. If
students could live in Chicago the year round and be trained,
how much more effective the Chicago Evangelization Society
would be.

Mr. Moody saw it also. And here the well-known story falls
in place as Moody and another man knelt on a vacant lot and
asked God to give it to them for a school. The trustees moved
swiftly as God answered that prayer, and bought property at
Chicago and LaSalle. In September 1889, came the formal
opening of the first building of the Bible Institute for Home
and Foreign Missions of the Chicago Evangelization Society.

A long name? Yes, but it cast a long shadow. The excitement of the dedication of that first building cannot be fully appreciated in the light of all the property that has since been acquired. The building was new, but it was crowded in with others along a dirty street without green grass or shade trees to make a campus. But its atmosphere was beyond description. Students went out with burning hearts to a world needing Christ.

Moody had no intention of using his school to compete with seminaries, for his students were not to pastor churches. They were to fan out throughout cities, taking the gospel to homes and shops and street corners. He wanted his students to know the Bible, to be able to teach others what was in it, and to use music. The masses were at one end of the ladder, the clergy at the other. His students were to bridge the gap—to be the rungs.

What made the school survive those first tempestuous years when it could so easily have folded? After all, there was no pattern to follow. Looking back at the events of those years in the school, the city, and the nation, it is clear that many circumstances combined to form the cradle to support the infant institution.

First, Miss Dryer and Moody and others had the vision and the courage to try a new thing. Then the times provided the need. A huge influx of immigrants came, responding to the poignant invitation on the Statue of Liberty: "Give me your huddled masses yearning to be free," but they became slaves to poverty. The economic conditions in the United States frightened people. The buildings at Chicago and LaSalle were not isolated in an ivory-tower atmosphere; they were within reach of infamous Haymarket Square; they touched slum areas. Thinking that "religion" might help when nothing else would, some rich people gave money to Moody whether they actually believed his message or not.

But there were other reasons for its success. Many Christians were uneasy as they heard Robert Ingersoll move up and down the country ridiculing Christ. Evolution, Christian Science, and other beliefs preached ideas remote from the redemptive work of Jesus Christ. Christians wanted a place they could count on. Mr. Moody had traveled the world and knew how easily reform replaced regeneration, how easily criticism of the Bible took away faith. So 2 Timothy 2:15 became the motto of his school: "Study to shew thyself approved unto God, a workman that needeth not to be ashamed, rightly dividing the word of truth." Hundreds and thousands across the country knew Moody as the man of the Bible, so they trusted his school.

Furthermore, Moody brought teachers and guest lecturers who were well known in this country, as well as famous men from Great Britain. Leading preachers such as F. B. Meyer, W. G. Moorehead, G. Campbell Morgan, Andrew Murray, C. I. Scofield, and A. J. Gordon gave their rich knowledge of the Bible. This helped build the school's reputation as an important institution.

Then, of course, Chicago's location made the city a center of leadership for all kinds of activities. It was easy to reach by train from anywhere. A school in the heart of the leading center of the Midwest could logically be expected to succeed.

The school benefited from Moody's years of actively supporting the Sunday school movement. The miles of travel and the countless speeches gave him a host of friends ready to support this new venture for God. Because the Institute was interdenominational, the YMCA, the Student Volunteer Movement, the American Sunday School Union, Christian Endeavor, and other groups cooperated with it. They sent students for training, and then used Moody graduates in their organizations.

The school succeeded because money came in to support it. There was never a surplus, but funds were always sufficient. Moody never hesitated to appeal to his rich friends. He wrote a specific, blunt request in a letter:

Will you and your wife take one student each in our schools
out here for 1891? It will only cost $150 each, and they can
report to you every thirty days how they are doing. . . . $150
will keep them hard at work for [365] days, and they will do
much good, and be learning all the time.[2]

Then he added, "My wife and I are each going to take one."
But Moody had a source that far surpassed solicited gifts.
Stories are endless of God's supply when human resources
failed.

Finally, students came because this was a different school.
A lot of people wanted to study the Bible who had no intention of becoming full-time Christian workers. So who were
they? They came from cities, farms, small towns. Some came
already knowing much about the Bible; others knowing only
that they wanted to know more. Some came who were too old
to start the long process of college and seminary; others
wanted to know how to witness to relatives and neighbors.
There were ministers and seminary graduates who wanted
the concentrated Bible study that the Institute specialized in.
Women came also: those planning to go to the mission field;
busy mothers who wanted to learn how to lead their children
to Christ; women hungry to know God's Word.

These were exactly the people Moody had in mind for his
school—and before he, Miss Dryer. They wanted Bible
knowledge, and the school gave it. The curriculum centered
around the English Bible. Students learned its structure, its
doctrines, its content, its individual books. They learned how
to use it as a text in personal study and as a sword in personal
witnessing.

And as students studied the Bible, they sang. Music and
the Word, the two vital ingredients of Moody's preaching
campaigns, were the breath of the school.

The curriculum's third feature was the actual mission work.
Students learned methods in class and then practiced them in

many different ways and places in the city. Moody knew that mixing learning *and* doing was a biblical principle. Knowledge alone could be sterile, and doing without knowledge could go off on strange tangents. Doing *for* God must grow out of knowing God.

Every student took all the subjects and could enroll at any time in the year since classes were held the year round. A student could come for two years or for just a few weeks. Board and room was just $3.50 a week, and there was no tuition.

The school did not begin fully developed with a formal course and catalog. Many things had to be experienced by trial and error. If an idea did not work, it was dropped. The few regular teachers were augmented by visiting lecturers. Whenever Mr. Moody was in town, he delighted the students with the vitality he brought into the lecture room. Sometimes he said impulsively, "Let's have a holiday," as on his birthday, when he took the students and staff on a sleigh ride. When he was in Chicago, he lived in the men's dorm and ate in the dining room.

But Bible knowledge, musical skill, and the mechanics of effective witnessing rang hollow without the extra depth the Institute required of its students. The 1895 catalog stated clearly:

> Great emphasis is laid upon a development and deepening of the spiritual life of the student. If any student should go forth from the school without a more intimate acquaintance with Jesus Christ, and more of the power of the Holy Spirit in his life and work, the Institute would have failed in his case at the most important point.

This purpose remained the heart of the Institute through all the changing years.

When the school began, a board of trustees loosely governed the work. Anyone could belong to the Chicago Evangelization Society who agreed with its objectives and could give financial support.

But more responsibilities came when the year-round work shifted the emphasis from just evangelistic outreach into the city to a more formal, structured work. As the school expanded, the board of trustees updated the organization and administration. Some developments took place almost overnight; others came gradually through the changing pattern of years.

In all this the original objective remained stable: "The object of the Chicago Evangelization Society shall be to educate, direct and maintain Christian workers as Bible readers, teachers and evangelists; who shall teach the Gospel in Chicago and its suburbs, especially in neglected fields." The "neglected fields" soon stretched far beyond Chicago as trained pastors, evangelists, and missionaries carried out the command of Acts 1:8.

The school was always the heart of Mr. Moody's vision. But once it was strong enough to stand alone, he looked for new fields to conquer. His energy flowed out in many directions. When Chicago began plans for the World's Fair of 1893, Moody immediately realized the Institute's strategic location and purpose. If Chicagoans were excited about the Fair, Moody was more so. He saw it as the opportunity of a century for Christians. People from everywhere would throng the city, and Mr. Moody plunged into plans to reach them with the Gospel.

He knew there would be many exhibits to compete for the attention of the masses who would come. He aimed to present the Gospel in such a way that visitors would flock to his "exhibit" with as much enthusiasm as they would to the garish or the spectacular exhibits.

His strategy covered every detail. He quickly added two floors to the 153 Building to house the additional students he knew would come. The Institute became the center to train workers who then fanned out across the city to contact visitors. Each night the workers returned to the 153 Building to personally report to Moody the results of their day.

Throughout the months of the Fair, evangelistic services were held in a centrally located church in each of Chicago's three sections, plus meetings in more than 80 tents, mission halls, and churches. Moody did not expect people to come to his meetings instead of the exhibits, but he did want to make an impact for Christ. And he did. So many people attended church on Sundays that many of the exhibits closed those days for lack of attendance. An estimated two million filled the churches and tents during the May to October Fair.

Random samplings of the records kept of those attending the many services throughout the city read: July 9—36,200; August 20—42,700; September 17—48,400; October 29—52,550. Many visitors went home different from when they came. They came to Chicago to gawk at the unusual sights in life; they went home with new life in Christ.

This was the time the Chicago City Council changed West Pearson Street to Institute Place in honor of the work.

Moody's vigor and enthusiasm saw opportunities everywhere he turned. Whenever he saw a need, he did something about it and tied each new venture to the Bible Institute. The Bible Institute Colportage Association grew out of a need.

Mr. Moody never forgot his lack of book knowledge. This memory spilled over into a desire for literature that would help new converts grow in their Christian life. But he could not find what he wanted. The evangelical books already on the market cost too much for many of his converts. And a lot of what was cheap was not evangelical; this included the dime novels one could buy anywhere.

Moody's reasoning was direct: if he could not find the kind of literature he wanted, the solution was simple—write and publish it. His goal seemed impossible, for he wanted books that were evangelical, well written, readable, nondenominational, and inexpensive. He had to write them and print large enough editions to make the venture pay. So the Bible Institute Colportage Association (BICA) began, a separate organization from the Bible Institute but under Moody's direction.

The BICA began boldly with *All of Grace* by C. H. Spurgeon, followed by Moody's *The Way to God*. The first edition of 100,000 copies of Moody's book sold for only ten cents each. Getting books into print at one-third the price of most other religious books was no problem since the publisher, Fleming H. Revell, was Moody's brother-in-law. Seven of the first eleven books of the BICA were Moody's sermons edited for publication by his son-in-law, A. P. Fitt.

The exciting possibilities of the Colportage Library gave a new scope to Moody's imagination. Here was another field to try out ideas. He pioneered in publishing paperback books of a uniform size and binding. And he innovated the idea of encouraging people in his meetings to sign up for books that had not even been written, to receive them automatically when they were published.

Moody's salesmanship experience and drive sent him out looking for customers. The idea had worked long years before with shoes; why not with books? So colporteurs, Christians who were eager to serve Christ and earn a little money at the same time, took books from door to door. Some students paid board and room expenses at the Institute from money earned as colporteurs. So eager were some students that they swarmed into an area and sold books at seven cents a copy instead of the usual ten cents, causing some friction with regular colporteurs.

This literature outreach consumed Moody's interest in the last years of his life. Literature went where a preacher could not—on the nightstand beside the bed; on the dining room table; in the hospital to be read in the long, lonely nights.

The forgotten men in prisons especially weighed on Moody's mind, and he aimed to get the printed page behind prison bars. He started a book fund and personally raised most of the money needed to send books and gospel tracts free of charge to chaplains in prisons and reform schools. Something different for Moody? No, he simply carried through on his basic conviction that rehabilitation was not enough. A redeemed heart was needed if reform was to endure.

But Moody's constant concern was that those who were redeemed should reach others. He thought about the many lay people who had time to study in the summer, but who would not come to Chicago. From this came the Northfield summer conference, patterned after English Keswick. The first conference in 1880 lasted ten days and brought about one hundred Christians together for Bible study.

But his conference at Mount Hermon in 1886 caught the imagination of the world as one hundred students pledged themselves to "evangelize the world in this generation." The next year even more students responded and the Student Volunteer Movement launched out in 1888. This complete dedication of students to foreign missions is startling in view of the critical ideas about the Bible coming from colleges and universities at that time. Yet secular historians agree that the great foreign missions impetus of the closing years of the nineteenth century resulted from Dwight L. Moody's impact on students.

Moody put his conference idea into miniature in Chicago by organizing classes in various parts of the city to teach people the Bible and music. Called "union classes" because they were interdenominational, they were an extension out into the city of the training given on Chicago Avenue. Again it was a case of going out to those who could not or would not come to the school.

After making his commitment to God secure as a young man, Moody had poured his life into many activities in Chicago. He was a humanitarian, giving to meet social and economic needs, and weeping with those who wept. He was an evangelist, preaching the power of Jesus Christ to save from sin. He was an educator, stressing the need to know the Bible in order to maintain a life pleasing to God.

In 1890 he wrote to a friend: "I am thankful to tell you that I have some splendid men and women in the field. My school work will not tell much until the century closes, but when I am gone I shall leave some grand men and women behind."

Later he was asked, "Do you consider the Bible Institute a success? If you were starting over again would you follow the same plan?"

He replied, "Yes, it has been a great success and a wonderful blessing. I would do the same again."

The Bible Institute in Chicago was a success any way one looked at it. It is difficult to give exact enrollment figures for these years because the school had no registrar's office and because some students came for only a few weeks out of the year. Records do show a report Dr. Torrey made for the year 1890 of 173 men and 80 women. By the end of the first decade, three thousand men and women had been fired to action by Mr. Moody's school. They had hurried back to homes, offices, factories, churches, and out to mission fields, able to "give a reason for the hope" they had in Christ Jesus in obedience to His word.

In the early years of the work, Moody constantly reminded people that his Bible school did not give seminary training. But more and more seminary graduates found they needed the Bible training the Institute offered. The original purpose of training "gap-men" for within-the-city missionary work expanded dramatically as students demanded training for a variety of Christian service.

Suddenly in 1899 God took away the human motivating force of the Bible Institute. Though warned by his doctor years before that he had a heart problem, Moody tried to keep pace with the unfolding opportunities—revivals, literature, summer conferences, the Bible Institute. At 62, in the midst of a busy Kansas City campaign, he became ill and returned to his Northfield home. But even in his extreme weakness his mind raced, making arrangements for the work he loved.

He gave the responsibility for the schools in Northfield to his son Will, and the Bible Institute in Chicago to his son-in-law, A. P. Fitt. The day-to-day work of the classes was already in the hands of the gifted educator R. A. Torrey.

When Mr. Moody first came to Chicago, his uninhibited methods of witnessing made him an object of scorn to some who dubbed him "Crazy Moody." But success followed most of his ventures. And, since the world uses success as a measuring rod of greatness, Moody became a respected figure in Chicago, across the country, and around the world. Always with his name went his message—the power of Jesus Christ to change lives.

The general reaction of people to his death clearly showed his place on the American scene. A warm letter of sympathy came to Mrs. Moody from President McKinley, so soon himself to meet death.

"Moody is Dead," read the front-page black headline in many evening editions across the country on December 22, 1899. For several days the papers were full of his life and activities and words and works. News stories and editorials paid tribute to him.

This is not the usual reaction of the press to the death of a Christian. But there was a dimension to Moody that many Christians miss. A chance remark years earlier, "The world has yet to see what God can do with a man completely yielded to Him," struck fire in Moody as a young Christian, and he became that man.

The Moody Bible Institute stands as evidence of this total commitment to God. Moody lived through an era of turbulence, tragedy, doubt, and change. Yet he laid the foundation of an enduring work. Dwight L. Moody's story will not end as long as students come to learn from God's Word at Moody's Bible school.

THE UNIVERSITY CAMPUS drowsed in the warm afternoon sunshine. Summer sounds drifted in through the open window. But the peace of the outdoors contrasted sharply with the young student's inner turmoil as he listened to the lecture. The respected theologian echoed the conclusions of the heavy textbook.

"The Pentateuch is not the work of Moses but of many authors"; "Two men wrote the book of Isaiah"; "Daniel is a late book, recording history rather than giving prophecy"; "One gospel writer copied from another."

Reuben Torrey listened to the familiar arguments he had repeated to others. Yes, the Bible was the Word of God; he believed that. But these higher critical theories about its origin carried weight. They had the ring of logic, if not of conclusive evidence.

He stared down at the words of Scripture, suddenly so clear on the page before him: "Thus saith the LORD."

The professor's voice faded as Torrey concentrated on the thought that rushed over him. If the Bible was God's Word, then man's theories could not be true no matter how logical they seemed.

He lifted his head and, like John Bunyan, felt the weight slip from his shoulders and his mind. Never again would he put man's word above God's Word.

2

R. A. Torrey: Stabilizing a Vision

EXCITEMENT, ANTICIPATION, and new resolutions fill the beginning of any new year. Certainly the new century held promise of great things. But tragedy clouded the anticipation, for the twentieth century opened ominously. The 1900 Boxer Rebellion in China revolted the world when its wave of antiforeign feeling slaughtered foreigners, including missionaries and many Chinese Christians. President McKinley's assassination followed almost immediately, making people wonder what the world was coming to.

Theodore Roosevelt moved into the White House, and his vigorous, impetuous personality stimulated the nation's imagination and sense of adventure. The Rough Rider hero of the Spanish-American War pushed reform efforts to give everyone what he called a "square deal."

Conditions in the country urgently demanded change. The texture of life underneath a surface optimism was a tangle of threads knotted with strife.

Drastic changes had swept the nation after the Civil War. The industrial revolution swallowed the country's predominately agricultural economy. Farmers furiously protested tariff regulations and price fixing for their crops. Farmers' alliances eventually brought reform but left terrific ill will.

The cities took the greatest impact of unsettled conditions. The shift of people from the hard life of the farm to what they imagined would be the good life of the city became a rushing tide that could not be stopped. Young people and whole fam-

ilies came with hope in their eyes, which soon turned to hope-
lessness.

This enormous influx to the cities in the early years of the
century created gigantic unemployment problems. City governments tried in vain to cope with the swollen population
and provide sanitation, education, fire and police protection,
as well as control vice, crime, and city official corruption.

Poverty corroded the facade of prosperity. The growing
population demanded large-scale production of goods, bringing new problems. The impersonal machine age turned
people into robots who worked from early dark to late dark
at the drudgery of confining, mechanical labor. The rapid
growth of huge trusts threatened to gobble the idea of free,
open competition. Even prosperous, middle-class Americans
feared the power of giant corporations that were controlled by
a few wealthy individuals.

At the same time, exciting inventions and better labor laws
marked the first four or five years of the new century. The
Wright brothers made their first successful flight at Kitty
Hawk, North Carolina, in 1903. The miracles of electric
lights, the telephone, the sewing machine, the typewriter, and
improved harvesting machinery eased life. Child labor laws
slowly squeezed through to guard children from becoming old
before their time. The laws said children were allowed to
work only 48 hours a week in factories.

On the surface, Americans appeared to be chiefly interested
in getting rich, respectable, and cultured. But social and religious issues bothered people, too. Evangelical Christians
faced opposing beliefs and wondered how to reconcile science
and technology with belief in a personal, omnipotent God.
Many found little help in their ministers who were trained in
seminaries which had swung away from belief in the infallibility of Scripture. Prosperity and poverty; science and religion—
could these opposites be resolved in this new century?

These same conflicts brewed in restless Chicago. The city boomed as the twentieth century got under way. The noise of construction reverberated constantly with the new, high buildings pushing up. Culture deepened as the Art Institute acquired new treasures, Orchestra Hall was dedicated, and the budding University of Chicago attracted students from close by and far away places.

But tragedy often struck, and a matinee fire in the Iroqoius Theater brought crowds to stand by in tears as they watched bodies being carried out. Six hundred people, many of them children, were trampled and suffocated in the frantic rush to locked exits.

Chicago was the setting for a novel, *The Jungle,* which revealed the foul conditions in the meat-packing industry. Fortunately this scandal was not swept under the rug, but resulted in the Pure Food and Drug Act.

The city cried for reform in the midst of what one visitor termed its "frontier mining-camp mentality," where anything one could do without being caught was legal. Crime and corruption mushroomed. A 1903 survey revealed the vice-riddled police force and showed how unsafe neighborhood streets really were. Red-light districts advertised blatantly. In fact, Chicago's vice district in the early 1900s was the biggest in the world. Visitors to the city sometimes disappeared without a trace; particularly naive, young girls lured by the promise of good jobs. They were only known about when grieving relatives came looking for them.

Books exposed the corruption. Newspapers agitated about it from time to time, forcing city hall to take action. But the relief was always only temporary, because greedy human hearts resisted reforms that cut profits of whatever kind. This confirmed Mr. Moody's conviction that reform was empty without the regeneration of the human heart.

But what of Moody Bible Institute, the name the trustees

now gave the school? What would become of it in this squalid setting as it faced the challenge and need of the new century without its strong human leader? Some feared for its survival. Mr. Henry Parsons Crowell said, "When he [Moody] died, it seemed as if the life had gone out of the Institute."

This could literally have happened. If a Chicago *Times Herald* editorial could mourn, "The greatest evangelist of the century has passed away," how much more was the loss to his friends and associates, those now responsible for the work still so new. Why did the Bible Institute not die? Because it was God's work, not Mr. Moody's. God had other leaders on the scene before they were needed.

Crucial problems faced everyone. Although Moody's death did not collapse the work, the time of transition brought confusion. Was anyone strong enough to follow Mr. Moody? Where did the work stand financially? Administratively? Educationally? Would students continue to come? Would money come in to buy food, heat the buildings, and pay the faculty? Most important, would it stand firm in its commitment to the Bible while colleges, seminaries, and churches fell away on every hand?

A firm answer came from Dr. Torrey. "Though Mr. Moody was the president and the leading spirit of the Bible Institute, our work will go on just the same."

God had blended Moody's energy and enthusiasm and creativity to found the Bible Institute. Now the times demanded a different leader; a discerner of events, a man alert to the winds that blew confusing doctrines across the land.

Reading documents and letters from those first years, one could speak of a power struggle taking place. Perhaps some did see the glory of stepping into the shoes of a leader like Moody. If so, God guarded against that danger. A man with personal glory as his sole motivation would not have survived those unsettled years when finances were precarious and the future of the work was uncertain.

Out of the capable men who could have become the next leader, why was R. A. Torrey the right man? The answer comes from his background. He was born into a wealthy home in New Jersey in 1856. His mother taught him the habit of daily Bible reading. He said, "I had read my Bible every day of my life, without a single exception, since I was thirteen years of age. I was taught to pray so early that I cannot remember when it was done."

But prayer and Bible reading were only habits to him, and he grew up with just a veneer of Christianity. During his college years at Yale he buckled under social pressure and became a heavy drinker. Then in his senior year he was saved, and entered Yale Divinity School after graduation. While a student there, Torrey got his first taste of personal work—later to be his whole life—during Moody's New Haven campaign.

But his college conversion had not completely settled the questions his inquiring mind kept asking. During seminary, intellectual doubts about Christ's deity crowded in. He said frankly, "The professors at Yale Seminary at that time were all orthodox, but I was not."

He had to settle his questions. "I did not always believe in His resurrection, but I went to work to study the evidence to find out whether it was satisfactory and conclusive or not. I found that it was; that Jesus really did rise from the dead, as recorded in the four Gospels. That conclusion carried everything else with it that was essential."

But he battled other questions. He developed admiration for transcendental thinkers who had a strong following during those years, and he read a great deal of Unitarian philosophy. He continued to study in Leipzig and Erlangen, Germany, under Dr. Franz Delitzsch. There he at last found rest in the certainty of God's Word and turned forever from the false stand of destructive higher criticism. This thorough exposure to both sides of the religious controversy of the day prepared him to speak against the tide of biblical criticism which grew stronger each year. His knowledge and convictions made him an able defender of the faith in his later ministry.

He never again wavered on this issue of the infallibility of Scripture. Later, when a question arose about inviting a man to speak at the Institute, Torrey replied, "I do not know him, but you say he is something of a higher critic. That is enough to settle it."

When Torrey returned from Germany, he became superintendent of the city missions in Minneapolis. There he learned another lesson in faith, though a different kind. In January 1889, he wrote, "It became evident that the Lord wanted me to give up my salary, which had been paid with great irregularity. I proposed to take the whole Mission work—rent, gas, everything—as a faith work."

He kept a diary through the year. Each month's account is filled with, "I had no money to pay the rent, so I went to the Lord"; "I did not have money even for carfare"; "The potatoes were gone, no meat, and very little in the house for supper. . . . I took it to God in prayer and found great rest. He supplied." And so the year went.

And from that year's experience, Moody asked Torrey to come as superintendent of the school in September 1889. As the school's first permanent Bible teacher and director of the Biblical Course, Dr. Torrey also had to develop the curriculum and oversee the practical Christian work program. His mind worked logically, never in a disjointed, haphazard way. As he thought through the Institute curriculum, he set up two tests as criteria: Will it please God? and, Will it help the student? Any decisions, any changes were based on those questions. Above everything, he wanted each student to have his faith in God grounded in the Word of God.

Mr. Moody's death ten years after Dr. Torrey came as Bible teacher brought the Institute to a crisis. On his deathbed Moody gave Mr. Fitt the responsibility for the total work of the Institute, which included raising money, overseeing business details, and administering policies. In addition, the school demanded full time attention.

Already on the scene, Dr. Torrey was the logical choice for leader of the school, though he did not have the official title of president. In Dr. Charles Blanchard's words, "God led Moody to Torrey," as a teacher so that Torrey was on the scene before he was needed to head the school.

Because he had faced complex theological issues from first-hand study and experience, Dr. Torrey was eager to strengthen the Institute's program. He wanted the faculty to instill in the students a knowledge of the Bible and the ability to use it in facing issues.

The school's success since its founding came partly from the variety of well-known Bible teachers who came as visiting lecturers. But Dr. Torrey saw two dangers in counting on guest teachers. Some of the visiting teachers differed strongly in doctrinal viewpoint which confused and unsettled students. The second was the danger of emphasizing men rather than God's Word. Students would come to hear a certain teacher's opinion rather than to gain knowledge from God in His Word.

Dr. Torrey saw the need for continuity in instruction. He wanted his faculty to think of the Institute as *their* school. He wanted to build a resident faculty who would give all their time and energy to training students.

But Torrey turned his attention to another love—the Practical Work Course which gave students experience in *doing* what they learned. Each student had five assignments a week in the afternoon or evening. Chicago offered such a variety of spiritually needy people that every student could find something he enjoyed doing or was good at. If not, he learned to do it anyway. Many tears of anxiety lay behind the words of witness on street corners, in hospitals, in missions, and in jails.

Dr. Torrey followed Mr. Moody's thinking that knowledge kept to oneself does no good. Moody students were to be like the lepers in 2 Kings 7, who said, "We do not well: this day is a day of good tidings, and we hold our peace."

Dr. Torrey's experience in mission work gave him a love for people, but this side of his nature did not always show. He was dignified; his eyes were piercing, tolerating no evasion. People often thought him cold and stern. But he had an inner warmth and an enthusiasm for personal soul-winning. His love was for winning people to Christ; cultured and educated, or filthy and diseased, it made no difference. He could kneel beside a drunk in a mission or explain the gospel at an elegant dinner table.

The Gospel Wagon idea originated at the Institute. Pulled by horses at first, the wagons held a small organ, a desk for a pulpit, and a few seats for a choir. The wagons drove through the city, stopping for fifteen- or twenty-minute meetings. This was a "gospel clinic," and reached thousands who might never have entered a church bulding.

But students did not have to go very far from their front door to see the reason for the school's emphasis on practical work. Just a walk in the neighborhood showed the appalling need surrounding them.

In later years the practical Christian work emphasis became a vital part of the total training rather than a course of study. Even now, while it is a requirement for graduation, it is also primarily a service rendered by students who visit in homes, teach Sunday school, hold mission meetings, and visit in jails, hospitals, and nursing homes.

In the Institute's witnessing outreach, women students particularly were guarded against the dangers lurking in the city. Zeal and caution, faith and common sense went together on assignments in dangerous areas.

So the work grew. By 1901, Moody-trained men pastored churches in rural areas and were missionaries in other countries. More and more students came who had college and seminary training but wanted the Bible, music, and practical experience they could not get anywhere else. Others came because Dr. Torrey's speaking and writing sounded a clear trumpet call to belief in the Bible as God's infallible Word.

Students came to study, and the Institute's aim was to prepare them for a life of service for God. It was exciting for the students. Some came from wealthy homes; others came with no family encouragement and no money. But that did not matter since everyone was treated alike—no one paid tuition.

Everyone was treated alike in another way, also. To keep down expenses, the household department hired very little outside help. Students did the work around the buildings, except the cooking. Each student did an hour of domestic work daily—though if you were a fast worker, you could sometimes do the hour's work in fifteen or twenty minutes.

One entrance requirement insisted that students be in good health. This was essential to keep up with the twelve hours of study, the regular lectures, the five assignments, the domestic work, and still have the time and strength to take in some of the cultural advantages of the city.

Each applicant had to have more than just the desire to do Christian work; he had to show some ability for it. The school's training often included knocking off rough edges and developing tact to match zeal.

In these years, Monday was a day off from assignments and classes, and students used it to catch up with both study and sleep. On school days the rising bell rang at 6:45, with breakfast at 7:30. From there the day was never dull.

Everyone met together for classes; men on one side of the room, women on the other. Teachers had no overhead projectors, no film strips, not even an old-fashioned blackboard. Students furiously took notes with paper and Bible propped on their laps. But they studied and sang and learned and enjoyed their years of preparation.

Women's suffrage was a strong issue across the land, and it

was hotly debated at school, especially the rare times when men and women students ate together in the dining room.

"Women were given brains to be used," and "Some women know more than some men," the women students insisted. And of course they could always go back to the origin of the school for confirmation of their claims. Had not Mr. Moody been in favor of training women, but reluctant to include the men?

Students came; the school program grew, and so did other parts of the Institute. The training school remained the heart of the work. But the Institute branched out in the years following Moody's death into areas that were distinct from and yet closely tied to the main purpose.

Moody did this himself when he started the literature work. By 1900, his Colportage Association was recognized as the publishing department of the Institute. Within the next few years over four million colportage books were in print. Making money was not the goal; reaching people with gospel literature was.

Colporteurs offered 104 different titles and distributed thousands of Bibles and Gospel portions. Free literature reached people in remote, needy places; sometimes in a lonely farm house, other times in the loneliness of a noisy Chicago apartment. Men in the armed forces, prisoners, lumbermen in the north woods, school children, and missionaries hungry for spiritual food—the BICA touched them all.

The *Institute Tie,* begun in 1891 as a biweekly "open letter" to alumni to keep them up on what was happening at the school, had to be discontinued several years later. Remember, from 1893 to 1894 was that black time of deep depression throughout the country. People had no money to buy food or shoes for their children, and could not give as they might want to.

But in September 1900, the *Institute Tie* reappeared as a monthly magazine. Mr. Fitt edited it as one of his numerous responsibilities, wanting to spark the interest of people who were not Institute alumni. He saw its possibilities to bring needed prayer and financial support.

The magazine followed a rather informal format until Dr. Torrey and Dr. Gray became coeditors in 1907. Then it changed from a chatty and inspirational news letter to a magazine style. The editors' knowledge and writing skills gave the magazine a wider appeal. Ministers could find sermon help in it, and the lay person could get answers to his questions about the Bible.

Then Dr. Torrey branched the Institute out in another exciting direction; not a tangent, but an enlargement of the basic purpose of teaching people the Bible. Mr. Moody himself had talked about the idea of a correspondence school, but nothing had been done.

Correspondence study was a new trend of the times. Dr. Torrey kept alert to developments in secular education. He knew Dr. William Rainey Harper of the young University of Chicago, who also had the vision of a correspondence school. While other established schools talked about the idea, Torrey did something with the study-by-mail idea and launched the Institute's Correspondence School. There were no courses, so he wrote them, one on Bible Doctrine and the other on Practical Christian Work. A student could complete the doctrine course in two years by just several hours of study a week.

Who could enroll? Anyone "of both sexes who cannot, for financial or other reasons, attend the Institute personally." When a student completed a course, he received a certificate of progress which was accepted for credit in the regular Institute Bible Course.

But when could a man, working ten to twelve hours a day find time to study? Dr. Torrey thought of that, too. He had the lessons prepared in sections that could be easily folded. In this way a student could study while traveling to and from work on the street car or on the recently completed elevated trains.

What came next in this ever-widening circle? Another school—the evening department. Of course, evening classes were not new to the work. There had been such classes in Moody's Northside Tabernacle from the very beginning of the Chicago Bible work. In fact, those first years classes *had* to meet in the evening to reach working people; that was their only free time. And until the formal opening of the first building in 1889, there hadn't been day classes that people could attend full time.

Part of the original purpose of the evening classes had been to teach new immigrants to read English by using the English Bible. Here again was the combination always present in Moody's work; the social and the evangelistic.

This original evening work apparently disbanded for a few years in the 1890s, that depression period. Then in 1903 the Evening Department began. Classes met four nights a week that year, with about 125 coming each evening. This changed to three evenings the next year. Bible classes met Tuesday and Thursday, with a music class on Wednesday evening. A student could complete the evening program in three years and receive the same diploma as a day school graduate. This was not an easy way to get a Bible school education because people had a very long working day.

Dr. Torrey also continued Moody's extension of the Institute out into the city with Bible classes. The 1904 school catalog describes the scope of the Extension Department:

> Evangelistic services and campaigns are planned and carried out with members of the Institute staff. Supplies are furnished for pulpits, pastorates, pastors' assistants, Bible teachers, superintendents of Sunday schools and missions, church visitors, singers, choir leaders, and almost every form of practical Christian work. The regular instructors frequently lecture and teach at conventions.

Like Mr. Moody, Torrey had influence that went far beyond the boundaries of the buildings in Chicago. He left his imprint in more than forty books and many articles. His book, *What the Bible Teaches,* was used as a text at the Institute. *The Divine Origin of the Bible* is a clear statement of the inspiration of Scripture, much needed in those days of attacks on the Bible.

This work was not Dr. Torrey's alone any more than it had been Mr. Moody's. Many others contributed, too many even to list. Mr. A. F. Gaylord, for example, became business manager in 1893 and had a hand in almost every area of Institute life from Mr. Moody's time up through Dr. Gray's presidency.

God added a special blessing to the work through a Chicago businessman, Mr. Henry Parsons Crowell. Mr. Crowell had not known Moody personally, but heard him preach once and carried the memory of his words. Since Crowell lived in Chicago on Rush Street not far from the Institute buildings, he could not help knowing of the busy life going on there. A successful businessman and a godly, active member of the Fourth Presbyterian Church, he was naturally interested in any thriving work of God.

He invited William R. Newell to teach a weekly Bible class in his home. This class revolutionized his life and his wife's. Already generous in their giving, the Crowells dedicated their money to God completely, and they poured it and their time and concern into the Bible Institute.

Mr. Crowell was elected to the board of trustees in 1901 and became president of the board three years later, holding this position for forty years. He regarded this not as an honorary position but as a working responsibility. During the years he invested more than his money and astute business knowledge; he gave himself as well in time and thought and prayer.

Mr. Crowell was a godly man, and a practical man as well. As a successful businessman he knew the importance of sound business principles in any work. Funds must be acknowledged

quickly and accurately, and wisely spent or invested for the
future. God brought him to the Institute at the time when his
business skill and common sense were desperately needed if
the work was to last.

During Mr. Moody's life, his wealthy friends had given
willingly to his many projects. The gifts usually were generous, $5,000 to $25,000 at a time, but were given to meet a
specific need, not regularly and systematically. Their giving
showed their confidence in him, not in the work itself. When
he died, some people stopped giving. Others held their gifts
back until they saw what plans were made for the school's
future. After all, nobody wanted to pour money into a building if the doors might suddenly close. It seemed to some observers that for several years no one was really in charge of the
work as Mr. Moody had been. Dr. Torrey was away on an
evangelistic crusade, giving directions for the work through
correspondence with Mr. Fitt and Mr. Gaylord.

Mr. Crowell and Dr. Gray faced each other across the bare
financial bones of the work and asked each other the hard
question: Was the school really worth the effort needed to
lay a stable business basis?

They began with the question of money because the Institute's important biblical stand would crumble unless its financial foundation was strong enough to support it.

Mr. Crowell was generous with his own funds. His letters
came regularly when he was out of town with the quiet nota-
tion, "Enclosed is a check from Mrs. Crowell and me." His
biographer quotes Mr. Crowell:

> It was the hope of Mr. Moody that his son-in-law . . . would
> be able to stand by after Moody's death. But Fitt went into
> business leaving Gray and myself in charge. I was elected
> president of the Board of Trustees. I remained president.
> We had about [290] students. As president of the Board of
> Trustees, I realized Moody [that is, the Institute] did not

have a number of reliable friends. It was necessary for me
to keep the Institute going *until it did have reliable friends.*[3]

But he did not want the work to depend on him and the
gifts of just a few wealthy friends. He pictured thousands of
interested people across the country who would support the
work on a regular basis. To him it was a simple, logical equa-
tion—people prayed more for the success of a project if their
money was in it. And Mr. Crowell knew that money alone
would not be enough; gifts had to come with the prayer
backing of the giver.

Mr. Crowell saw something else just as clearly. The financial and prayer support should combine to hold the Institute
true to its purpose. If the purpose of training men and women
in God's Word ever faltered or swerved, the support should
stop. As he put it, "if the fire no longer burned, the Institute
deserved to die."

Back in the 1870s when the Chicago Bible Work first began
with Miss Dryer, a board of trustees had governed the work.
Later, Mr. Moody himself had been accountable to the board.
When Mr. Crowell became the president of the trustees, he
saw the value of a smaller committee elected from the board,
which would act on Institute business affairs between the
regular board meetings. So the executive committee was born.
Naturally, through the years these members of the board have
had the closest interest in the Institute's development.

The trustees and administration faced a real crisis in the
first years of the new century. Bills came regularly even
though income did not, and debts piled up. Something had
to be done about the buildings. New ones were needed to
care for the increasing number of students applying for admission. The existing buildings needed plastering, painting,
and rewiring as all old buildings do. The Iroquois theater
fire sent fire inspectors throughout the city with stringent
safety requirements—which cost money.

Drastic steps were needed, and the board made a decision.

From now on the Institute would pay its way as it went along. This meant no new buildings would go up, no large project begin unless the money was available to finish it. Was not this the place to apply the Lord's parable in Luke 14 about the man who began to build a tower and ran out of money? This executive committee had no inner vision to look along the years to see the campus of today, but they had the conviction that God's work required God-honoring practices.

If individuals could learn to live by faith as Dr. Torrey had during that year in Minneapolis, so could organizations. Repeatedly through the years when the economy kept people from giving, the trustees simply reduced the operating budget.

Did this mean a cutback in salaries? Unfortunately, yes. Heating? Sometimes. Food? At times students had reason to grumble. But money was not tied in debts, and when financial crises eased, the work expanded again. After all, the Scripture taught wise stewardship of money. If the Bible was the basis for classroom instruction, it should also be the basis for the financial affairs of the Institute.

It was the school that particularly needed Mr. Crowell's wise counsel in the months of financial and leadership uncertainty. Since the other parts of the work were tied to the school, they suffered when it did. While Mr. Moody was alive, even when he was not in Chicago, everyone knew who gave directions. But now no one person filled his shoes, or could, or even seemed to want to. Mr. Fitt had so many responsibilities to oversee, he could not give the training emphasis the attention it needed. And he gradually felt led out of the Institute into private business.

Someone suggested that Dr. Torrey, Dr. Gray, and Dr. C. I. Scofield should serve as deans and divide the responsibility. Each man would take turns teaching four months a year on the Chicago campus and have the direction of the school during that time. The other eight months he would travel, filling the many demands the Extension Department received.

This plan did not work out, partly because Dr. Scofield did not come to the Institute at all. Dr. Gray was on the spot as a Bible teacher. But he and Dr. Torrey were both strong, opinionated persons, and did not always agree on policies. Since Dr. Torrey had been at the Institute on a regular basis during Mr. Moody's time, he seemed the logical person to have the final say about the complexities of the school. But in 1901 he went to Australia for an extended evangelistic crusade.

While he was gone, so many big and little problems arose that could not be handled by slow mail from far-off places that Dr. Torrey wisely resigned. Mr. Crowell then urged Dr. Gray to accept the top administrative position on a full-time basis.

It is a little difficult to sort out the titles of positions in these early years. Dr. Torrey came to the Institute originally as superintendent of the school. He kept that title when he briefly stepped into Mr. Moody's position. During this time Dr. Gray's title was *dean,* and he kept this when he succeeded Dr. Torrey as head of the school. At that time the title *president* referred to the president of the board of trustees, Mr. Crowell.

Mr. Crowell, the businessman, agreed with Mr. Moody, the evangelist, about the relationship of social reform and individual redemption. One could not stand apart from the other.

The Institute lived in the heart of a city known far and wide for its vice and crime. These were the years the city's exposé showed how open the red-light districts were. Mr. Crowell knew of the loan sharks' power to ruin small businessmen. He read the city's survey on vice and corruption and vowed to act. He took steps first through his church. When that proved too slow, he formed a Committee of Five with other concerned businessmen to force city officials to act. The committee pressured the mayor to order places of prostitution closed and to take action against other forms of organized crime, which wove a tight net around its victims. The committee got results, but they were only temporary. The octopus-like tentacles of sin chopped off one place simply reached out to another.

Mr. Crowell practiced his Christianity in these civic enterprises, but his heart beat with the work on LaSalle Street. Dr. Houghton eloquently described Mr. Crowell's quiet, dedicated years of service.

> Without wishing to take anything from the records of past Institute leaders, in all honesty the admission must be made that this man has been more responsible than any other for the success of the Moody Bible Institute from early times to this . . . hour. The continuance of the school, the sending forth of multitudes of young people with the gospel to the ends of the earth, the radio ministry, and all the other varied activities, were made possible largely by the devotion and generosity of this consecrated servant of Christ.[4]

But much of that was still in the future in 1903-4. Institute leaders looked back to the day Mr. Moody knelt on the vacant lot and asked God to give it to him for a school. God answered; buildings went up, students came, and the school grew.

Mr. Crowell and the men he gathered around him as trustees assured its financial stability. Dr. Torrey put the curriculum on a firm educational basis and fixed a strong practical work emphasis. Through his writing and speaking, he made the Institute known as a place firmly committed to the Word of God.

The Institute urgently needed this double foundation of financial and theological stability. The world stood at the edge of a dark tunnel of spiritual and economic depression, with no light evident at the other end. Moody-trained men and women faced the challenge of being lights in the terrible period that lay ahead.

HIS FRIEND'S SPIRITUAL POISE haunted the young pastor's memory. But the secret of that spiritual depth seemed too simple. Could just *reading* the Bible over and over and over again do that for a person?

James Gray picked up his Bible. He would try it. He would brush up on his Hebrew and Greek and read directly from the original to get the intricate shading of each word. After a while he sat back, perplexed. He felt no sense of peace. He was working and studying, but the Bible was not speaking to him as it had to his friend.

He resolutely opened his English Bible and read Genesis through without stopping. Then he went back and read it again, and again. Excitement quickened as the outline of the book became clear. Its message and meaning stood out as never before.

Exodus was next, then Leviticus, and on, through each book in turn. Each book was a separate jewel in its own perfect setting, but each fit the next and all reflected the radiance of the message of God.

This *was* the secret of knowing the Bible; simply letting it become a part of his very being.

3

James M. Gray: Defending a Vision

PRESIDENT THEODORE ROOSEVELT'S energetic enthusiasm infected the entire country with confidence as the century got under way. He pushed for a great variety of social and economic reforms, and searched for ways to make the United States a recognized leader in the world.

Many events made these years memorable. Another spiritual revival on college campuses sent many young people to the mission field. But in the same year, shock waves reverberated from Einstein's theory of relativity because it seemed to contradict long-held concepts of time, space, and motion.

Newspapers headlined startling advances almost daily. People avidly read of the mass production of those Model-T cars they once had derisively ridiculed, and of Robert Peary's breathtaking expedition to the North Pole, and of those foolish, risky airplanes.

The great era of railroads sounded mournful train whistles in big and small cities from east to west. Minimum wage and hour standards were set for women and children in spite of dire predictions that such idleness could bring only trouble. Immigration reached its peak between 1900 and 1910, intensifying the country's labor problems.

Peace movements, supported by churches, talked enthusiastically about the Millennium. Delegates from 33 denominations gathered excitedly in Philadelphia to form the Federal Council of Churches. Unfortunately, this council blurred important differences in belief, implying that many broad paths led to God instead of the one "narrow way" of the Bible.

Even while Moody was founding his Bible school, slight winds of theological change were blowing, gradually shifting attitudes. Now the winds became gales that swept away traditional, familiar ideas. The Social Gospel movement was one of these, and it grew tremendously. Many people agreed with the philosophy that it was more important to do something for man on earth than to spend so much time talking to him about heaven.

People could not help being optimistic as the century began. Medical discoveries brought freedom from pain and disease. Jobs and better wages gave freedom from poverty— if you were ambitious. The old idea still held that if you were poor, it showed you were lazy and not really trying to get ahead.

People generally had more goods, more money, more labor-saving devices, more leisure time. And all of it apparently came from man's own ingenuity. If man could do this by himself, did he really need God? Maybe the old idea of man's depravity was wrong; maybe he *was* essentially good. Of course there were the poor, but even the Bible said they would always be around. And as for the crime and vice, it was just better not to read the scare stories in the newspapers.

The trouble in the world seemed remote. In spite of the *Lusitania's* sinking in 1915, the war across the water was a long way off. So Woodrow Wilson was reelected, because he "kept us out of war." Almost immediately American boys sailed for Europe. The peace fervor evaporated in the flood of emotion that billed the fight as a moral war fought for a righteous cause.

Former optimism about man's goodness faded as the war's end brought depression and disillusionment. Americans gave generously to organizations that tried to feed the starving, helpless victims of the war in Russia and other European countries. But the most powerful attitudes in the nation were isolation and suspicion of foreigners. The overriding desire was for peace without being a part of other countries' problems. Congress made clear this mood of isolation by defeating President Wilson's dream of America's participation in the League of Nations. The terrible flu epidemic of 1918 that killed more Americans than the guns of war had killed soldiers, took the heart out of the most optimistic.

An era of hate and fear began that spread through the following years. Suspicion of foreigners showed in malicious ways. Ku Klux Klan activity increased. Anybody who was not clearly a white, established American heard the jeers and ugly names and sometimes felt the stones. The unreasoning hysteria resulted in a mandatory literacy test which kept from the polls the immigrant who had not learned English. Finally in 1920 a quota law severely curbed immigration.

The country seemed to turn in on itself after the war. People wrapped themselves in their own problems and were blind to the growing danger of totalitarian governments across both oceans. Liquor became a consuming national scandal. The 18th amendment passed after a bitter struggle, and prohibition became law in 1919. The intent of the law was right, but too many ordinary citizens found ways to get around it. This triggered a sharp rise in crime and a general lawless spirit. The speakeasy and the bootlegger became a shameful part of American life.

Though the war and its sorry aftermath shattered some people's confidence in their ability to control their own destiny, it did not force them back to the God of the Bible. Sociological thinking and scientific writing remained basically anti-Christian.

Many factors shaped the doubting, cynical spirit and kept people from the earlier, simpler faith of their fathers. For one thing, city life separated people from the church. Many found it hard to get started in a new church when they moved to the city. There was no social pressure to go to church; your neighbors did not know—or care—whether you attended or not.

But it was not just not attending church that turned people from God. Getting *things* became a national obsession. And when people got them—the automobile, golf clubs, more leisure time—they were too busy using them to think of God.

Then the discoveries in the sciences turned men from God. The Scopes Trial in Tennessee in 1925 dramatized how deeply Charles Darwin's evolutionary theories had penetrated national thought.

Of course religion did not escape the doubts. "Yea, hath God said . . . ?" seemed to be the question asked everywhere one turned. The authority of the Bible was the main issue in the fundamentalist-modernist division that tore the 1920s. Established denominations with creeds based on the Word of God crumbled before this new spirit that intellectually pitted man against God and found God wanting. Modernism reached its peak in American Protestant churches from the 1920s to the 1930s. Abroad, Karl Barth and Emil Brunner began their long domination of the theological scene, their influence infecting America's religious outlook.

Evangelicals were naturally alarmed at the denial of basic Christian doctrines by ministers and seminaries. Some reacted with shrill denunciations, but many able evangelical preachers and teachers held their ground during these tempestuous years. They did not bury their heads in the sand nor take an anti-intellectual, irrationally angry stand. *The Fundamentals,* a series of twelve booklets, gave a clear explanation and a defense of essential Christian doctrines. Dr. Torrey and Dr. Gray were two of the scholars who presented the conservative view of Scripture in a scholarly, reasonable way.

During these years faith missions were established. Other Bible schools and Bible colleges joined Moody to vigorously challenge the teaching in schools originally established by Christians.

But it cannot be denied that the liberals had the loudest religious voices in the 1920s and 1930s. Other groups and cults busily pushed their ideas as well. Christian Science added thousands of converts, and Russellism spread. Emile Coué's host of followers faithfully repeated his slogan, "Day by day, in every way, I am getting better and better." All these attitudes were based on the belief that God was not sufficient, and that man could do better for himself by himself. Church attendance declined during these years, and the peak of missionary activity passed.

It was also an age of human heroes: Charles Lindbergh with his solo flight from New York to Paris; Babe Ruth with his home runs in baseball; Will Rogers with his unique sense of humor. Even gangsters like Al Capone had admirers.

The 1920s was a distinct segment of time bounded by the war at one end and the depression at the other. Called the Jazz Age in newspapers, and glamorized in fiction, particularly by the F. Scott Fitzgerald stories, it critically questioned the Puritan heritage Americans had lived by. The radio, movies, the automobile, increased leisure time; all these affected people's habits and attitudes.

George Bernard Shaw, H. G. Wells, H. L. Mencken, and other writers mocked Christian virtues. Traditional moral values crumbled as the divorce rate soared, and gangsters openly defied the law. The Jazz Age was really a continuation of the Gilded Age with a shallow materialism covering poverty, bigotry, and credulity. Americans seemed almost fanatical in pursuing both business and pleasure.

Then came the dark October day of 1929. Thousands of America's banks and businesses failed, and Europe's economy collapsed also. Nothing that President Hoover tried, worked. The poor from coast to coast faced the cold winter huddled in

"Hooverville" shanties made from flattened tin cans and tar-paper, and searched garbage cans for food.

In July 1932, the Bonus Army of 7,000 desperate army veterans marched on the capital. The march only dramatized all that was out of joint in the country. Those who had offered their lives to their country in war found they were not wanted in peace. In early 1933 nearly fifteen million unemployed stretched across the nation. It was "the worst of times" as the nation stood on the brink of calamity.

The good and the bad in the nation in the early 1900s intensified in cities like Chicago. Large-scale tragedies made headlines more frequently. The excursion ship, the *Eastland,* sank in the Chicago River in 1915, killing more than 800 people. Somehow those dead seemed more real than the bodies strewn on faraway battlefields.

The extremes of wealth and poverty in the city clashed often during the 1920s, bringing violent confrontations between labor and business. But a worse conflict came in connection with employment needs. Industry needed workers to fill the jobs men had dropped to go to war. Women took some of the places, but others were still open. Negroes hurried from the South, hoping to find work. So many came that they spilled out of the neighborhood boundaries they were expected to stay within. Chicago did nothing about the potential problem, and it finally boiled over in hot July 1919 in a murderous white-black confrontation.

Besides this, the excesses of the Roaring Twenties reached a crescendo in Chicago. Even school children knew about the houses of prostitution and the gambling dens. Mr. Crowell's original Committee of Five became a Committee of Fifteen as other businessmen joined the effort to control the appalling vice. Chicago became the center of a vicious era of control by gangsters. Al Capone's mob squeezed the city government, even intimidating or corrupting police. No business or industry was exempt from paying tribute to gangsters in one way or another. Guns blazed to settle gang feuds in broad daylight on the city streets. It seems unbelievable that some Chicagoans, otherwise decent people, took pride in the city's reputation. Many made it easy for gangsters to monopolize the city because of their own disdain of the prohibition law.

Of course other things, good things, happened in these years. The Burnham Plan gradually made the city beautiful, parts of it at least. The lakefront developed with the Field Museum, the Shedd Aquarium, the Adler Planetarium, the Museum of Science and Industry, the Wrigley Building.

Some of the city's streets were a maze. Though Chicago had put through a uniform street numbering system early in the 1900s, the old joke that "you can't get there from here" was so true it was not funny. So the Burnham Plan straightened and widened streets, among them LaSalle Street. While the automobile moved people out to the suburbs, blocks of elegant apartment buildings towered along Lake Shore Drive where the rich and influential found refuge. But tenements still spread their decay on the west side of town.

Chicago's symphony orchestra busily built its reputation. Parks welcomed picnickers. Golf, baseball, tennis, and swimming were all available to Chicagoans.

The city's size and growth and vitality were described by Carl Sandburg, who called Chicago the "city of the broad shoulders." And to the casual observer, the buildings did spell security and permanence.

Then the foundation of society abruptly crumbled, and the economy crashed in on the city. Even though the financial crisis was so bad in 1930 that the police were not paid, the Century of Progress Fair opened in 1933. Chicago hoped the money that the throngs of visitors spent would cure its depression. It didn't. The Palmolive Building beacon lighted by President Hoover in 1930 was all that flickered in the dark years ahead.

How did the Moody Bible Institute survive these disastrous years, facing the depression and doctrinal apostasy that sapped energy from people and organizations? Instead of driving people *to* God, the depression developed an indifference in them. The Institute could not solve the financial crisis; that was not its mission. But a stand against apostasy was.

The Institute stood, as it had under Mr. Moody, on the fact that personal salvation through Christ alone was the only absolute answer to any problem. Though its human leadership changed, the Institute's purpose to train men and women in the Word held firm.

The work required a strong leader. Dr. James M. Gray's wisdom carried him and the Institute through the cataclysmic events of the war, the frenzy of the Twenties, and past the low point of the depression. One reason for Dr. Gray's success was his complete disinterest in pushing himself. "Whom am I serving?" was the question he asked himself continually.

A line in one hymn he wrote reads, "I'm only a sinner, saved by grace." Reticence was such a strong characteristic that there is little biographical detail about him. He seldom spoke of himself and rarely used himself or his family as personal illustrations.

He was born in New York City in 1851 and was saved as a young man. He accepted a call to a church in Boston in 1879 and remained there for twenty-five years in a strenuous biblical ministry. While a pastor, he also taught the Bible courses at what is now Gordon College.

Dr. Gray strongly valued his citizen rights and took an active part in community affairs. He was an ardent prohibitionist and vigorously supported anti-liquor legislation, because he felt that preaching against sin meant actively working against it.

While a student in New York, Dr. Gray heard Moody preach many times. Dr. Gray sang in a choir at the Hippodrome meetings. Later Moody asked him to speak at the

Northfield summer conference. There Dr. Gray covered the lengthy, and to some incomprehensible, book of Job so clearly and interestingly in one lecture that the layman could understand. This impressed Moody, who then invited Gray to teach the Bible classes at the Institute while Dr. Torrey was away in summer conference work. He wrote Dr. Gray in May 1898:

> During the next four months while you are at the Institute I want you to understand that you are in Mr. Torrey's place as superintendent. Mr. Gaylord, Mr. Newell, Mr. Towner, and Miss Strong will, I am sure, give you loyal support in their different departments; and I hold you responsible for the conduct of the institution, not only in matters of teaching but also in general.
>
> The Institute is very dear to my heart, and I believe a mighty work can be done there.[5]

That fall Mr. Moody wrote Dr. Gray again, planning for the next summer, and added, "I think [last summer] was the best summer of all the nine years that have passed."

During his years as pastor, teacher, and evangelist, Dr. Gray developed his gift of teaching the Bible clearly. He was frequently asked to lecture on, "How to Master the English Bible." This method of synthetic study and of reading and rereading the Bible had been a turning point in his life, and he wanted it to be for others also. His conviction that the Bible was the Word of God remained the foundation of the Institute in these years of continual drift. The 1922-23 school catalog spelled this out plainly.

> The English Bible is the great and fundamental textbook. It is felt that simply from an intellectual point of view a clear and comprehensive acquaintance with its contents is in itself a liberal education. But from the spiritual side, to know it thoroughly and to be able to handle it rightly in preaching, teaching and in personal work is absolutely indispensable to Christian workers of every class.

Therefore, in the curriculum of the Institute, everything gives place to the Bible. No matter how well trained a student may be in gospel music, for example, or in any form of practical Christian work for the home or foreign field; no matter how deep his spiritual experience or how fervent his zeal in soul-winning; no matter what natural gifts or qualifications he may possess, if he be not grounded in the Word of God he cannot be an entirely safe leader among men, nor can he truly glorify God in his service. It is in this department of its instruction more than in any other that the motto of the Institute finds application: "Study to show thyself approved unto God, a workman that needeth not to be ashamed, rightly dividing the word of truth."

The Bible is taught by different methods, but the design is by one method or another to cover all its books within the cycle of two years.

Dr. Gray came to the Institute to teach the English Bible. When he became the dean in 1904 on Mr. Crowell's urging, he was both teacher and administrator. At that time the Institute's condition was shaky. Mr. Moody was gone. Dr. Torrey had been in charge for a few years and now he was gone. Those who supported the work began to question: Was this to be a pattern of instability?

But Mr. Crowell's confidence held steady then and during the lean years that followed. Sometimes already meager salaries reluctantly had to be cut. Other organizations, churches, and businesses defaulted on their debts after World War I. Moody managed. Even through the severity of depression years, monthly salary checks came through regularly. Only one month in all those years was a check delayed a few weeks, was the memory of one faculty member.

Faculty, students, and staff met regularly for prayer the first Tuesday morning of each month. But when the Institute faced a particularly urgent crisis, classes and work stopped, and everyone joined in a day of prayer. For several years these were frequent.

Dr. Gray continually showed his interest in his staff. It is true that some complained his watchful eye saw too much. But his watchfulness included his hammering at the board of trustees about salaries for the staff. He well knew that the Institute elevator operator was hard pressed to stretch her 28¢ an hour wage. His concern for others' welfare finally caused Mr. Crowell to remind the board:

> We have discussed the salaries of all the members of the faculty and the employees of the Institute in relation to the high cost of living, but so far not a word has been said about the Dean. . . . He may be so much of an "optimist" that he can make a dollar go farther than other men, but even if that be true, it is not right to longer refrain from increasing his salary.[6]

Money came from unexpected sources during these years. When increased automobile traffic forced the city to widen LaSalle Street, some Institute buildings were left almost out in the street. The city reimbursed the Institute in cash, which was used to demolish some old buildings and to plan for new ones. The Women's Building at 830 North LaSalle was cut off fourteen feet in front to take it back in line with other buildings along the street.

The Education Department, the heart of the work, was Dr. Gray's main concern as the administrator of the Institute. He made the weekly faculty meetings important as he drew the faculty into the problems and needs of the school. To Dr. Gray they were a team working in close partnership. Sometimes the faculty could object that Dr. Gray demanded they be too close a team because he insisted they live near enough to be present at Institute functions. But when Dr. Gray and Mr. Crowell had faced each other at the low point and discussed the basic needs of the work, they had agreed that a strong faculty was essential to its growth. The work needed fresh, alert, forceful teachers; not tired men. So Dr. Gray demanded a full measure of devotion from the faculty and other employees.

Dr. Gray's leadership expanded the original courses Mr. Moody had begun with such zest. This was not a change in purpose, but just a steady marching to keep pace with people's needs. The part of the curriculum that remained constant was the emphasis on the Bible, music, and practical Christian work.

The first major change in the structure of the courses combined the separate Men's and Women's Departments. (Though men and women still sat on separate sides in classes and the dining room!) That year, 1905, also marked the first graduating class of four men and three women.

English was added to the curriculum. This previously had been a basic feature as part of the original evening classes to help immigrants become Americans and to teach them the Bible.

When the Bible school began, academic qualifications for entrance were minimal. A common, or grade school education was sufficient. And this was all the education the masses of people had. Many intelligent, self-educated people had not been able to go beyond the fifth or sixth grades. Free high schools were common in most states after 1876, but attendance was not compulsory. But this was changing in the twentieth century, and higher standards were demanded in secular education.

Dr. Gray wanted to guard against the idea that the Institute's minimal entrance requirements meant that the training was inferior. But his proposal to require high school education and to include English as a required subject brought a storm of protest. Even Dr. Torrey was fearful that this would keep out those for whom the school was intended in the beginning.

But Dr. Gray held firm. He wanted Moody graduates to have more than a basic knowledge. A man of precise grammar and clear diction, he wanted his men and women to excel not for themselves, but for the sake of the Gospel. God's message was too important to be carelessly handled. Moody graduates should be so well-trained that they would be respected by those who were educated. Excellence was Dr. Gray's goal, however a student might dread some courses.

In 1916 the written objective of the Institute was "to educate, direct, encourage, maintain, and send forth Christian workers, Bible readers, gospel singers, teachers and evangelists competent to effectually teach and preach the gospel of Jesus Christ."

What else was this than an application of Acts 1:8, recognizing that the scope of the training began in Chicago and then spread worldwide.

Mr. Moody's original conviction had reechoed through the years. "It is not the aim of the Institute to do the work of the theological seminaries, but rather to aid and supplement them." But the changes in the country's religious climate made changes necessary in Institute thinking. The tremendous increase in the nation's population from 1900 on obviously meant there were more unchurched people. This meant more ministers were needed. At the same time, seminaries were not graduating enough men to fill the vacant pulpits or to organize needed new churches. Worse still, those schools that no longer stood for the inspiration and authority of Scripture produced ministers whose trumpets gave the uncertain sound Paul warned against in 1 Corinthians 14:8.

Because Moody's school was well known across the country for its biblical stand and its expertise in Christian work, men students began pleading for pastoral training. The need made an answer imperative. A course in pastoral theology was added to the curriculum. Within just a few years the content of the Pastor's Course, which had expanded to three years, sounded

like the curriculum in a seminary with its Greek, Bible ex-
position, church history, practice preaching, theology, and
church polity classes. But these courses were additions to the
existing curriculum. The emphasis remained on equipping
students for a variety of Christian service.

An interesting sideline of those years was the arrangement
the Institute had with the Swedish Evangelical Free Church
to train young men wanting to be ministers in that denomination. Eventually the program became a separate work, and
still later developed as Trinity College and Trinity Evangelical Divinity School.

Another forward step in 1917 put Dr. P. B. Fitzwater as
registrar, relieving faculty of the details of admitting students
and keeping records. This made for more accurate reporting
of student enrollment and added to the school's efficiency.

Then another first: the Jewish Missions Course added in
1923 trained workers to reach Jews with the Gospel. Moody
is still the only school offering a three-year course in Jewish
studies.

The city of Chicago was the mission field to the original
Chicago Evangelization Society. But as the perspective of the
school broadened, that seemed a limited view, like looking
at the world through a keyhole. These were the days before
specialization on mission fields, and the missionary had to be
a jack-of-all trades. The missions course enlarged, offering
new subjects and including medical training. Of course this
was not in-depth training, but it was sufficient so that a
Moody-trained missionary on a lonely outpost could survive
himself and treat the diseases of his people. Manual training
classes gave missionary students know-how in laying cement
or building a house.

Then, as though Moody himself were there to start impulsively down a new path, the Institute reached out in the
Christian Education field. The little mission Sunday school
had given Mr. Moody his first taste in serving Christ. Because

of his deep interest in Sunday school, the International Sunday School Lesson became part of the Institute's first curriculum. At that time colleges and seminaries had no Christian Education departments. The Sunday school course at the Institute was the forerunner of Christian Education departments in other schools of higher education.

Once again developments in the nation's religious climate affected Moody's curriculum. Liberal thinking gradually influenced the whole Sunday school movement. When the International Council of Religious Education organized and made clear its doubt that the Bible was God's infallible Word, the Institute severed connections with it. By then Moody's Christian Education program was strong enough to stand alone in training directors of Christian education, at that time a new vocation in Protestant churches.

The Institute did more. It took a bold step and invited representatives from other Bible schools to meet in Chicago and discuss ways to standardize what they were all teaching. The result was a new organization, the Evangelical Teacher Training Association (ETTA). The Institute's influence and reputation was so strong that the ETTA recommended to other schools the curriculum and textbooks Moody used in its classes. These textbooks, written by Dr. Clarence Benson, were based on Dr. Gray's synthetic method of Bible study. All that the Institute had built so carefully through years of trial and error now was the basis for building in other schools.

Mr. Moody had pushed Sunday school because it was the only place some children were learning about the Bible. But sometimes that instruction was terribly inadequate if teachers were poorly trained and if the material was not well written. Also, many churches used denominational materials written out of the doubts in the nation's theological controversies.

Since this was often the case, Dr. Benson was burdened to improve Sunday school materials. He began to develop a new system of lessons, using his students, some of whom were college graduates with teaching experience. After eight years of writing, trying out the lessons, and then rewriting, the All Bible Graded series of Sunday school lessons was ready.

They had to be published. The Institute did not want to get started publishing Sunday school materials, so Scripture Press was born, a spinoff from the Institute. Like a breath of fresh air, the Scripture Press lessons were based on the Bible, adapted to the age capacity of the pupil, and very practical in application.

While all this was going on in the Christian education area, major changes were taking place in the total education department. Dr. Gray's insistence on top quality meant constant reevaluation of the curriculum. Sometimes courses were kept as they were because they met a need. If they did not, they were combined with other courses or dropped altogether.

H. L. Mencken's biting accusation that "any illiterate plowhand, if the Holy Spirit influences him, is thought fit to preach," was too inclusive. It did not take into account institutions like Moody that combined scholarship and evangelical fervor. The Institute aimed for high academic standards without diluting the spiritual emphasis.

1925 brought another forward step in curriculum reorganization, and the music department received the impetus. Music had been so vital in Moody's evangelistic campaigns that he had made it an essential part of the very first classes. But now a distinct three-year music course made it possible for students to specialize in voice, piano, or organ. Before this, music majors had to complete their training in a conservatory or a music department in another school.

But Dr. Gray loved music and wanted the students to be so well trained at the Institute that they would raise the level of the average church music program—which he considered to be disgracefully low and so dishonoring to the Lord.

The Institute's musical training was not restricted just to those with ability. All students, even those who were definitely unmusical, had to take some music course. Naturally, not everyone appreciated this, and some dreaded the music hour that required them to lead a song.

The first choral group at the Institute came from a practical situation on the campus. Dr. Gray had a regular Sunday afternoon service in the school auditorium as an example to Pastors' Course men of a well conducted church service. Music was an important part, and Dr. Gray asked the music department to provide a choir of Institute students. This began the Auditorium Choir, which sang for these services and later branched out in concerts in Chicago area churches. Later choirs widened even more the school's reputation for excellence in performance and in the quality of the music.

When Dr. Gray assumed the title of president of Moody Bible Institute in 1925, he merely continued the responsibilities he was already carrying. From then on, the title *dean* referred to the dean of the education department. At this time Mr. Henry Coleman Crowell became assistant to the president, continuing his father's interest in the work.

All student life concerned Dr. Gray. Sometimes students thought he took too much interest, that his eye saw too much. Those late to chapel felt his stern look follow them to their seats and heard him say, "You have an engagement with the Lord, and you dare not be late."

But he saw the students as his responsibility to teach and protect. He never hesitated to send memos on their behalf. For example, one went to music teachers: "The private music lesson of a student is not to be interrupted by the teacher taking personal telephone calls. The student is paying for his lesson and deserves full value." Or, one to the household department: "Put a light over the door on the northwest corner of the corner building. That is a dark area, and one that is dangerous for our women students."

Dr. Gray firmly believed in exercise and worked to have a gymnasium built so the student's physical development would match his mental and spiritual training. Students were not required, but expected to have forty-five minutes exercise every day in the open air. Many of them got this rushing to and from assignments.

Even though tuition was free, many students needed financial help, especially in the hard years after the first World War. So Dr. Gray urged an on-campus Student Loan Board and an Employment Bureau. Local businessmen were eager to hire Moody students, because they could be trusted. During the depression years only part-time jobs were available, since so many men with families to support walked the streets looking for work. But students found odd-jobs as janitors, chauffeurs, clerks, night watchmen, and elevator operators. The household department still depended on student help to cut its costs, so one part of the Institute helped the other.

Dr. Gray's years as president spanned the great changes in the country's attitudes, ideas, morals, and fashions. Naturally these changes were reflected in the Institute as well. Frequently the administration had to ask, "Shall we go along with this, or shall we stand firm?"

Some decisions were easy to make. At first, students at the Institute from the Chicago area could live at home except for the final term, when they had to be in residence. As more dormitory space became available, all students were required to live in the dorms except married men with families.

But this opened another problem, the sensitive problem of race. It was particularly sensitive in Chicago after the 1919 riot. Regretfully, black applicants were told they must find housing outside the dorms.

Other difficult issues were faced. Dr. Gray was concerned that in spite of the extremes in the fashions of the day, Moody students must keep a standard in appearance and behavior. Fashions for women changed radically from the pre-World War ankle-length dresses to the flapper era of short skirts, rolled silk stockings, and heavy makeup. Where to draw the

line? Naturally students and administration sometimes
clashed. If Alexander Pope's little verse were ever quoted:

> Be not the first by whom the new is tried
> Nor yet the last to lay the old aside,

students would have thought the administration seldom vio-
lated the first line and never broke the second!

We look back and smile at the "sleeves to the elbow" rule.
The girls then did not all smile of course, and some found
ways of getting around it. One could always put elastic in the
sleeve and pull it up or down as the situation required. And
the men grumbled at wearing coats and ties in the dining
room in Chicago's blistering heat. Life was regimented, but
after all, was not this the "West Point of Christian Service"?

Two sisters came for the music course intending to stay for
the summer term only. They were vivacious and had heard
reports of the rules. One of them said, "The rules were ridic-
ulous, but, oh, the spirit of the place! You couldn't find it
anywhere else." And they stayed the full two years and graduated.

Single students were not the only ones who needed looking
after. The married ones did also—and so did their wives.
Families were uprooted from quiet, comfortable, familiar surroundings and dumped into Chicago's dirt and clamor. Classes
and study assignments and employment consumed the husband's hours. But the wives felt the loneliness and emptiness
of their days. So Mrs. Gray organized the Married Women's
Guild. She knew from experience all that was demanded of
a pastor's wife and wanted these student wives to be ready to
help their husbands. In Guild they learned Bible study methods, Bible doctrine, Christian education, personal evangelism.
They practiced leading meetings and giving devotions. They
learned to sew and to be better mothers. They exchanged
money-saving ideas and recipes. And they shared with each
other the lessons God taught them. While the mothers were

in class, the children were cared for in a nursery staffed with Institute students. Mrs. Gray's program was unique and remains so, for no other school provides such an opportunity to student families.

The energy of the education department did not stop with the day school. The evening school continued as an essential part of the program. In the early years evening school students could room and board in the dormitories just as day school students did. Those living in the city who came directly from work could buy a supper of meat, potatoes, vegetable, bread and butter, coffee, and desert for twenty-five cents.

For a time during the 1920s, the evening classes duplicated the day school curriculum. But as the day school courses expanded, it was impossible to offer them all in the evening. By 1930 an evening school student who wanted to complete any course other than the General Course had to enter day school for some of the subjects. This narrowed the evening school objective back to its original purpose of training laymen to work in their local churches but not necessarily as full-time workers.

What was happening to the Correspondence School during this time of tight money and war scares? It grew. While deep in depression and tossed about by the swirling controversy over Scripture, people still demanded Moody's courses. These courses were not experiments but gave well written, clear instruction. In 1912 Dr. Gray's *Synthetic Bible Study* course joined the three already available. Then in quick succession came a brief *Introductory Bible Course,* a course in *Christian Evidences,* and one in *Evangelism.* The fourth significant addition was Dr. Scofield's important three-volume *Scofield Bible Course,* which covered the entire Bible. Courses multiplied in missions, church history, teacher training, and Bible study.

Dr. Torrey pioneered the whole study-by-mail idea. Now the times were ready for another step, the class study plan.

People could still enroll as individual students, but they could also study as a group under the supervision of a leader who sent the exams in to the Institute for grading.

Another innovation was the "Radio School of the Bible" in 1926, at the very beginning of the Institute's radio outreach. But this belongs in that part of Moody's exciting growth. It is enough to say that the Institute's study-by-mail-by-radio was the first of its kind anywhere.

Mr. Moody's desire to put literature behind prison walls had dominated his last few years. Now in the mid-twenties, a correspondence course changed the life of a prisoner. In 1926, the Institute magazine ran his eager testimony:

> Eight years ago, I was arrested for forgery, and was sentenced to a state prison. . . . Many tried to show me the way of salvation, but everything sounded too hypothetical for my materialistic mind. I have finally arrived at that blessed point in my life when a man is truly born again. Truly the study of God's Word shows us the way. It has brought me to a complete right about face.

This sparked a response in readers who sent in money to provide free courses for prisoners.

While the schools experimented and expanded, other parts of the work grew also. Students do not end their Institute ties when they cross the platform to receive their diplomas. The present, thriving Alumni Association doesn't show its small beginnings. Moody alumni keenly felt the "tie that binds," especially those in far off places. Graduates eagerly read news of classmates in the Institute magazine and sent in their own news items. But an alumni association was not formed until 1916 when Dr. Fitzwater and Mr. Gaylord pushed the idea, and got enthusiastic response from former students.

The extension work of the Institute touched former students and graduates. A staff of experienced Bible teachers and musicians were busy the year round, holding city-wide meetings as well as individual church meetings, and winter and summer conferences. In spite of the liberalism of the day, Christians hungered for teaching from the Word, and the Institute stepped in to help local pastors.

Founder's Week is one of the best known Institute-sponsored conferences. From Moody's impulsive "It's my birthday, let's go for a sleighride" beginning, the observance of his birthday grew into a significant week-long spiritual oasis. In 1911 a week-long observance marked the Institute's 25th anniversary, although regular classes met each morning. Then in 1919, Founder's Day was observed as part of a five-day conference whose theme centered on what part evangelism should play in the post-war years. The next year the conference was advertised as the Founder's Week conference and has continued since except for the year when the widening of La Salle Street made so much remodeling necessary that crowds could not be accommodated. The Extension Department works with the president to promote and carry out the many details of the meetings. Those attending the conference see only the top side of the tapestry—the smooth blending of music and messages. The underside is the mass of detail—phone calls, letters, tight schedules, and sometimes explosions of frayed tempers: all forgotten in the blessing of the conference.

The Extension Department also helped to place graduates in pastoral and teaching positions as well as other areas of Christian work. An intriguing statement in the school catalog in these early years said that there was no lack of employment for Moody-trained students: this meant places of service after graduation.

In 1924 the Extension Department took on the third job of raising funds for the Bible Institute and its related ministries. Mr. Crowell's principle of building a broad base of support from many friends continued. The donors were the key to the Institute's financial stability.

But the money did not just float in. A staff of men traveled in almost every state, calling on long-time friends of the school, people who had known Mr. Moody, and making new friends. The money came as direct, one-time gifts, through monthly pledges, by annuities, trusts, and bequests. There never was a surplus, so the money had to be stretched, used, and invested wisely. This part of the extension work was built on the scriptural principle that should underlie all giving to God: "Freely you have received, freely give."

There is something else to remember. Stewardship men give as well as get. In those difficult years their calls took them to lonely, discouraged, poor, troubled people to whom they gave spiritual counsel, comfort, and encouragement.

Another part of the Institute's work felt the unsettled times. The *Institute Tie* went through a series of name changes until in 1920 it became the *Moody Bible Institute Monthly*. Some argued that this was a mistake because the name would turn people off. It may have turned some off. But it also gave fresh courage to Christians surrounded by liberal theology after World War I. Here was a magazine that took a stand on current theological and social issues and spoke courteously but boldly. Naturally it would—it was another voice of Mr. Moody's school.

Under Dr. Gray's leadership the magazine broadened its contents and included articles on a variety of subjects, offering something for everyone. Articles faced up to current issues, poems and sermon illustrations gave inspirational help. Mission field news kept people abreast of happenings overseas, and questions ranging from, What's wrong with Unitarianism? to, Were the ninety and nine sheep saved? were answered. There were book reviews and news of former students. Even for a time, there was a column giving help on how to get the best reception from radio receivers.

Something new under the sun developed in the early 1920s; something exciting—radio. Mr. H. C. Crowell was one of the first to catch the vision of what radio could do. He was eager to make bold use of this new way to expand the Institute's program. But naturally there were problems. Money was the most obvious. In 1926 the depression had not yet hit the country, but at the Institute, funds were always tight and had to be carefully measured out for essentials, not for extras.

Then money came unexpectedly, marked for the specific purpose of broadcasting. This seemed to be proof that radio was to be one of the necessities. Not everyone was easily convinced of this, including Dr. Gray.

But another impetus came almost accidentally. Several Moody students had been hired to play their cornets at a display booth in the Chicago Furniture Mart. The musical talent that Station WGES expected to come for a broadcast could not make it because of a sudden, violent storm. The Moody students filled in with hymns, and the grateful station gave the Institute an hour's free time each Sunday evening.

Then on July 28, 1926, WMBI was born, with a two-hour service of dedication, its theme song, "I Want You to Know Him." A *Chicago Tribune* reporter wrote of the "pure tone" of this new station and of its "technical perfection."

A report in the November 1927 Bulletin tells what lay behind this technical perfection.

> The studios where the microphones are located are in the Men's Dormitory of the Institute, and near at hand is the large Auditorium which is also used for many of the programs. The programs are carried by wire from these studios to the amplifier room, which is situated on the top floor of the Women's Building. This means that all communication between the announcers in the studio and the amplifier room must be by telephone and signal lights.
>
> From the amplifier room special telephone wires go out to the transmitter at Addison, Ill., nineteen miles from Chicago, where the program is actually "put on the air." It can be readily seen, therefore, that the voice originating in the

studio goes into the microphone, through the wires to the amplifier room where it is magnified and sent out over special telephone wires to the transmitter at Addison, from which it is broadcast.

At first WMBI broadcast just six hours a week, with two hours each in the morning, afternoon, and evening. But being on the air did not solve all the problems; it opened more. All radio stations at that time had to prove their value to the public, and the facilities had to meet government standards. Mr. Coleman Crowell took the responsibility of working with officials in Washington and with the Federal Radio Commission so that the Institute followed government regulations strictly. As always it held to Mr. Moody's principles of being innovative and quick to seize opportunities for God, and yet doing so as men accountable to Him.

In 1928 the Moody Bible Institute Radio Station Corporation charter gave as its objective: "to preach and teach the gospel of Jesus Christ, as set forth in the Bible, by spoken message and songs, accompanied by instruments of music, and to stimulate men and women to Christian service." The few broadcasting hours over a leased station had multiplied to many hours broadcast over the Institute's own station in just two years.

The response to that first 1926 broadcast was unbelievable. In fact, just after the program, Dr. Gray was amazed to receive a letter from a listener in Florida. Other letters of appreciation poured in immediately from as far away as Texas. One family in northern Minnesota let their small children stay up to hear the midnight hour broadcast. A wider geographical listening range was possible in those years because there were fewer stations and less interference.

The letters that came helped determine the type of programming, and the station moved rapidly from mainly musical programs to a wide variety to appeal to housewives, children, shut-ins. Listeners studied the Bible through the "Radio

School of the Bible." Foreigners heard the gospel in their own language—Swedish, Norwegian, German, Polish, Spanish, Italian, French. The walls surrounding shut-ins dissolved as they listened. The station reached out with hope during the depression years, reminding listeners of the "Bread of life" available to the hungry.

Dr. Gray's original hesitation about using the radio in the Lord's work quickly evaporated. He wrote Mr. Crowell in 1928, "It would gratify me to see the Institute . . . asserting the rights of the Son of Man over the air, which He created."

The Institute's primary aim was to use this new medium to reach listeners with the Gospel. A second aim was to build a broader base of support for the Institute by bringing listeners into the Moody family. And this is what happened. Even during the early years of the thirties when depression bit into donors' ability to give, money came in for the radio ministry. Many other small, struggling stations were forced off the air for lack of funds. All through the economic crisis, WMBI's good financial base, fine equipment, and capable staff impressed Washington officials. Who could doubt it was of God?

Dr. Gray used every opportunity and means possible to broaden and deepen the work in Chicago. But his influence did not stop there. Both speaking engagements and writing carried the impact of this reserved, unassuming man far beyond the bricks and stones of the buildings.

Dr. Gray's skill with words and his incisive mind were needed at this time to explain and defend the Word. Darwin's theories and other liberal, rationalistic ideas affected the thinking of the average man-on-the-street. This doubt and skepticism had faced Moody to some degree and Dr. Torrey even more, but not as strongly as now in Dr. Gray's time. No one doubted Mr. Moody's allegiance to the Word. But he had not needed to defend the authority of Scripture, and he was not as prepared to do so.

Now questions regarding the inspiration and authority of

Scripture spread like a prairie fire in churches and among ministers trained in liberal seminaries. Here Dr. Gray used his knowledge, his skill in writing, his deep understanding of Scripture, and his awareness of the implications of false teaching to speak out in defense of the truth.

Church people reacted in different ways to higher criticism. Some who claimed faith in Christ surrendered to liberal thinking. Others tried to harmonize their traditional faith with the new theories of doubt. But many others firmly rejected the higher critical views of Scripture. This was the stand of the Institute, which showed its position in many ways.

In 1914, at the outbreak of World War I, the Institute sponsored a Prophetic Bible Conference at Moody Church. Ministers from across the country gathered to pledge belief in the fundamental doctrines of Christianity. As an outgrowth of the conference, the Institute restated its own doctrinal position in the 1915-16 catalog.

1. We believe that the Bible is the Word and Revelation of God and therefore our only authority.
2. We believe in the Deity of our Lord Jesus Christ, that He is very God by whom and for whom "all things were created."
3. We believe in His virgin birth, that He was conceived by the Holy Spirit and is therefore God manifested in the flesh.
4. We believe in salvation by divine sacrifice, that the Son of God gave "His life a ransom for many" and "bore our sins in His own body on the tree."
5. We believe in His physical resurrection from the dead and in His bodily presence at the right hand of God as our Priest and Advocate.
6. We believe in the universality and heinousness of sin, and in salvation by Grace, "not of works lest any man should boast"; that sonship with God is attained only by regeneration through the Holy Spirit and faith in Jesus Christ.

7. We believe in the Personality and Deity of the Holy Spirit, who came down upon earth on the day of Pentecost to indwell believers and to be the administrator in the church of the Lord Jesus Christ; Who is also here to "reprove the world of sin, and of righteousness, and of judgment."

8. We believe in the great commission which our Lord has given to His church to evangelize the world, and that this evangelization is the great mission of the church.

9. We believe in the second, visible and imminent coming of our Lord and Saviour Jesus Christ to establish His world-wide Kingdom on the earth.

10. We believe in a Heaven of eternal bliss for the righteous and in the conscious and eternal punishment of the wicked.

Furthermore, we exhort the people of God in all denominations to stand by these great truths, so much rejected in our days, and to contend earnestly for the faith which our God has, in His Holy Word, delivered unto the saints.

Any question about the necessity of such a detailed restatement dissolved with a look at the social and religious conditions of the day. Many sprang to the defense of the Scriptures with hot, angry words. Dr. Gray used his pen as a sword to refute, correct, and instruct forcefully but gently. When some answered critics with rash statements, Dr. Gray's answers were balanced and scholarly. This reflected to the benefit of the Institute.

A reporter at one of Dr. Gray's meetings wrote:

With charming courtesy he can look his hearers in the face and say personal things of a sort rather humiliating to the modern man, without stirring up the pagan elements of revolt. I should say that he had cultivated gentlemanliness as a fine art; and that he demonstrates the proposition that truthfulness and courtesy are, when combined, more forceful than truthfulness without the latter quality.[7]

Even though he was calm and reasonable, Dr. Gray's defense of the historical, biblical fundamentals of the faith was uncompromising. He spoke directly in articles, editorials, and pamphlets. During his years in Boston, he saw firsthand the insidious hold of Christian Science on sincere, earnest people. He wrote *The Antidote to Christian Science,* which did not attack the people, but the belief.

It was a different story with Harry Emerson Fosdick, a man who denied the faith he was ordained to uphold. Dr. Gray's *The Audacity of Unbelief* gave a vigorous, scalding reply to Fosdick's *The Peril of Worshiping Jesus.*

Other titles reflected his concern for the issues of the day: *Why I Believe the Bible Will Stand; Why a Christian Cannot be an Evolutionist; Spiritism and the Fallen Angels; Modernism a Foe to Good Government.*

When the postwar push came for an "inter-church world movement," Dr. Gray spoke out for denominations. Moody Bible Institute's faculty, staff, and student body was interdenominational, but united in the bond of fellowship in Jesus Christ. Membership in a church was a requirement for entrance, and students were encouraged to become involved in a local church while in school.

Another side of Dr. Gray shows in the heritage of songs he left. Some of the most widely sung are: "Nor Silver Nor Gold"; "Only a Sinner"; "What Did He Do?"; and "Bringing Back the King." Every school has a school song, and Moody is no exception. The "Christian Fellowship Song," written by Dr. Gray and Dr. Towner in 1909 says, "God bless the school that D. L. Moody founded; firm may she stand though by foes of truth surrounded"—an apt description of the day.

When Dr. Gray became the Institute's leader in 1904, horses' hoofs still clip-clopped on brick-paved streets. This gave way by 1934 to the clang of streetcar bells and the roar of the automobile. Chicago bustled energetically in spite of being deep in the throes of depression. Dr. Gray's wisdom

guided the school from the uncertainties following Mr.
Moody's death, through the hard times of the war, past the
shallowness of the twenties, into the controversies swirling
around the Bible, and partially through the Great Depression.

Many man-made schemes surfaced briefly during those
years of prosperity and war and depression. Most had failed.
As Dr. Gray's presidency drew to a close, another attempt was
made to buoy people's spirits by the Century of Progress Ex-
position, which opened in Chicago in 1933. Thousands of
visitors poured into the city, but its value was as fleeting as
dew in the hot morning sun. The depression ground on. The
world's future looked grim in 1934.

But the work of Mr. Moody and Dr. Torrey and Dr. Gray
flourished. Not in money, but in enthusiasm. The Institute
facilities grew, the curriculum strengthened, the outreach
broadened, the student body increased. And Dr. Gray finished
his job.

Someone once said of him, "Men grow and do their work in
their appointed time," but that's not a sufficient epitaph for
Dr. Gray. God undoubtedly added to it His "Well done, good
and faithful servant."

CREATOR OF IDEAS
Sketches, Monologues, Comedy Song Parodies, and all Kinds of Stage Material, Written to Order

THE YOUNG ACTOR stepped back and surveyed the advertisement with satisfaction, rubbing his hands together. That should bring results.

The ad did bring results; but not satisfaction, not lasting happiness. A nagging emptiness, a sense of loss remained after the curtain fell and the applause faded.

Will Houghton knew the emptiness was inside, in his heart. He had heard too many of his mother's earnest prayers for his salvation. He knew the emptiness would grow unless he stopped pretending life was satisfying and surrendered himself to God.

Finally he yielded. And in yielding, he exchanged his own ideas of creative success for God's eternal creativity in his life.

4

Will Houghton: Nurturing a Vision

THE ECONOMIC STORM rumbled ominously just over the horizon and broke in 1929. The national picture in Dr. Gray's closing years as president was grim.

March 1933 was the low point in the nation's morale as unemployment figures soared. Bread lines shuffled men along cold sidewalks in city after city. No one was prepared for the shock of the depression that boiled out of the world's failure to settle its economic problems after World War I.

The 1930s live vividly in history books and memory as the Great Depression, a time of frightening oppression by poverty. It is true that some had money reserves, and for them life went on as usual. But millions of Americans lost money, homes, joy, courage. Some threw their lives out windows of high buildings or jumped in front of trains.

Farmers watched the topsoil of their farms blow away in fine dust or stared grimly at the two cents per quart they got for milk. Two hundred thousand Americans left the futility of home and lived in hobo jungles while they looked for work. Desperate for work to stay alive, city people and farmers, family men and teenagers rode freight trains across the country at the risk of jail by the police or death at the hands of fellow travelers.

The depression paralyzed the nation. The poor, as usual, had nothing. But along with them, the hard-working middle class lost its thriftily earned savings. No combination of private agencies, no churches had enough resources to cope. Only the government could do it. President Franklin Roosevelt, new in office with his "The only thing we have to fear is fear itself," tried to exorcise fear with a bundle of name agencies he called the New Deal.

Some of these gave outright, immediate relief—money, food, shoes. But some of the government agencies made work. Men who had no other way to keep their children from crying with hunger got jobs with the Public Works Administration (PWA) and the Works Progress Administration (WPA). These jobs helped unskilled laborers, electricians, plumbers, artists, and writers to keep the wolf outside the door. The Civilian Conservation Corps (CCC) took young men from 18-25 off the street curbs and put them to work in camps planting trees and constructing dams. From 1933 to 1936 a variety of New Deal legislation kept families from falling apart by providing income and hope.

In addition, old-age and unemployment insurance began, and the Social Security Act was passed in 1935. Banks reopened gradually, business began a slow recovery, and confidence seeped back. Many benefited from the public aid; some could not have survived without it. But many others opposed what they saw as the creeping influence of government in daily life, fearful that the New Deal would discourage free enterprise. The controversy that began then over the "welfare state" never went completely away.

In spite of the depression terror that faced families, many found simple ways to be happy, and some children grew up never knowing they were poor. Families depended on one another, and neighbors found they needed each other. The radio brought *One Man's Family* into homes, and up and down streets millions laughed at Jack Benny, Fred Allen, and Fibber McGee and his closet.

Unusual events caught people's interest in struggles to survive: the Dionne quintuplets were born in 1934; Will Rogers and Wiley Post crashed in Alaska in 1935; Britain's King

Edward abdicated in 1936; and that year Jesse Owens infuriated Hitler by his outstanding Olympic record; Amelia Earhart disappeared over the Pacific in 1937; in 1938 Orson Welles' "War of the Worlds" broadcast sent thousands into the streets in terror.

During the thirties, other forces shaped the country's attitudes and actions. These were philosophical and religious rather than material or political. These forces did not hit as sharply as the depression, but they had a lasting influence on American culture and religion.

The decline in moral values of the Jazz Age coupled with the flood of gangsterism and lawlessness alarmed many. The repeal of prohibition in 1933 was a bitter blow to Protestant groups which had pushed for the original legislation, thinking it would control liquor.

Uncertainty eroded the relative quiet between the wars. Scientific advances left many feeling insecure, particularly during the depression when both unskilled labor and professional people walked the streets in ragged shoes, looking for work. What good were telephones and cars if one could not afford them?

The Social Gospel movement seemed to some to be right after all in preaching that this life needed more attention than the afterlife. Many churches joined in condemning the social order and even advocated more extreme measures than the New Deal was taking. New groups formed during these years. Frank Buchman and his Oxford Movement reached "up-and-outers" with a do-good philosophy.

Intense preoccupation with their own needs, and a strong spirit of pacifism blinded Americans to the totalitarian threat developing abroad. Paralyzed by their own problems and insulated by a mood of neutrality, they did not want to see what was happening in Europe and in Germany particularly.

And a spill-over of the cancer in Germany tinged honest American isolation. Gerald B. Winrod, Gerald L. K. Smith,

Charles Coughlin, and others spewed violent anti-Semitism along with extreme nationalism and drew many thousands of followers. Then the holocaust of war broke over Europe.

Though the spirit of isolation continued, the government began a gradual buildup in defense preparations. By December of 1940, President Roosevelt warned that America must be the "great arsenal of democracy." Defense needs provided more jobs, and this helped bring an end to the depression as the calendar turned over to the forties.

Then Japan bombed Pearl Harbor that day in December 1941, and the nation entered the war to protect national security and to stop totalitarian aggression. For the next four years the country poured all its energy into the war effort, which completely ended the depression.

While Europe staggered under devastated lands, a crippled economy, and millions dead at war's end, the United States came out undamaged and prosperous. Nothing could bring back some of its brave young men, but many returned to pick up life once more.

The neo-orthodox movement in theology rose out of the circumstances shaping these years. It stressed a return to the Bible, but not a return to the doctrine of scriptural inerrancy.

Consistently, evangelicals stood undaunted for the reliability of Scripture and the need for personal salvation through Jesus Christ alone. The Inter-Varsity Christian Fellowship in the mid-thirties tried to answer college students' questions about Christianity and bring together Christians on secular campuses for fellowship and encouragement. Youth for Christ did the same for high school young people. The National Association of Evangelicals (NAE) was formed in 1942 to give evangelical churches a united voice with the government such as the liberal Federal Council of Churches already had.

The chaotic economic, social, and religious conditions in the nation affected churches in different ways. Some closed entirely during the unsettled times; others merged to conserve buildings and programs and finances. Still others found attendance increased as people searched for meaning to their hard life.

The depression bit deep into Chicago's economy. Companies failed, "no help wanted" signs filled windows everywhere, bread lines lengthened, men tried to support families by selling apples and pencils on street corners. The city had no money, so it paid its employees in scrip, and some months teachers did not get paid at all. In warm weather entire families crowded Grant Park, curling under newspapers to sleep. When the weather turned cold, shacks of old boards and flattened-out tin cans lined the lake shore. Old men huddled, homeless, under newspapers on the lower level of Wacker Drive, some dying there from cold and hunger.

The city organized relief agencies while private institutions and individuals and churches gave food and clothing. Some restaurants set out special garbage cans of leftover food that would have been thrown away as scraps in ordinary times.

The depression halted the vigorous construction boom of the 1920s. Although the New Deal program provided funds for building projects in the thirties, recovery came slowly, with only the Merchandise Mart and the Field Building added to the famous Chicago skyline.

Chicago resumed its role of host to political conventions as Franklin Roosevelt was nominated for president in 1932. During this time the isolation feeling in the rest of the country ran high in Chicago as well. Then Roosevelt's 1937 dedication of the Outer Drive Bridge became a major foreign policy speech as he warned of the mounting aggression in Europe.

The outbreak of war abroad interrupted the Chicago Plan Commission's goal to improve living and working conditions in the city. All the energy now poured into the defense effort.

In the midst of war fever, one of the most significant mile-

stones of all time took place in Chicago. Dr. Enrico Fermi
completed the experiments that had consumed his thinking,
and he and his associates put together the atomic reactor under the old football stadium at the University of Chicago.
The implications of this successful test were not clearly understood by Chicagoans or the world until August 1945, when
the mushroom-shaped cloud hung over Hiroshima and ended
World War II.

During the dismal depression days, the work on LaSalle
Street searched for a new leader and found him in Dr. Will
H. Houghton.

Little is known of Dr. Houghton's growing years, for he
seldom spoke of them. He was born in Boston in 1887. His
godly mother, a widow early in her marriage, prayed earnestly
for her son's salvation, wanting him someday to be connected
with the work Mr. Moody had founded. Though he was
saved when he was fourteen, it was not until he had been a
professional actor for several years that he yielded to God,
who changed his life around completely. He attended Eastern
Nazarene College in Rhode Island for a brief time. Later
Wheaton College and Bob Jones University awarded him
honorary degrees.

Soon after Dr. Houghton dedicated his life to God, Dr.
Torrey invited the young actor-turned-preacher to the Mont-
rose Bible Conference as soloist and song leader. Though
Dr. Houghton had little formal theological training, his association with Dr. Torrey and other outstanding preachers of
the day deepened his love for the Word. No one, listening to
his messages, could doubt his knowledge of Scripture or miss
his evangelistic fervor.

But tragedy came to him in 1916 during his first pastorate
in Pennsylvania, when his wife died after two years of marriage, leaving him with two young children to care for.

This personal sorrow came just at the time the nation

plunged into World War I. Houghton served as a chaplain in army camps and was sent to a camp in New Jersey to counsel soldiers before they shipped out to battlefields across Europe. God used him there as He had Mr. Moody in similar circumstances long years before.

But God did something more; He gave Will Houghton a new life partner. The terrible flu epidemic of 1918 struck down soldiers in training camps as it did civilians all across the country, and women were needed to assist in the army camps. The YWCA asked Miss Elizabeth Andrews to go to the New Jersey embarkation camp. She went to help—and found love. When she married Will Houghton, she joined her own distinctive abilities to her husband's and shared his years of ministry.

While a pastor again in Pennsylvania, Dr. Houghton wrote four tracts which struck response in Christians across the country both for their courageous stand for the truth and for the author's clear, incisive writing. The tracts, reprinted again and again, began the effective writing ministry which Dr. Houghton carried with his duties as a busy pastor. His main emphases in all the churches he served were evangelism and Bible study.

In 1930 Dr. Houghton became the pastor of the well-known Calvary Baptist Church in New York City. From there the Institute board of trustees called him in 1934 to succeed Dr. Gray as president of the Institute.

From a human viewpoint this was not an enviable position. When the national economy hit rock bottom the year before, the Institute felt it keenly. Income fell off drastically, because people simply had nothing to give, much as they might want to.

The work itself looked impressive with nine hundred students in the day school, a thousand in the evening school, and ten thousand enrolled in correspondence courses. And the radio, the magazine, the publications, and extension meetings kept the buildings alive with activity. But none of this would continue without money.

With depression lying heavy across the country, only one course of action remained. The new president's first act was a call to prayer, asking the support of students, alumni, and friends.

> Believing that God alone is equal to the needs of the world today, and that only He can equip the Moody Bible Institute to meet its increasing responsibilities in these difficult but significant times, we hereby urge every friend of the Moody Bible Institute to set aside certain hours for intercessory prayer in behalf of the Institute. It is suggested that Friday, January 18, 1935, be designated our Day of Prayer, and that on that particular day groups of Alumni and friends gather in the homeland or on mission fields to spend time in united praise and intercession. We would suggest for special concentrated prayer the hour from 12 to 1 noon, Central Standard Time.
>
> We would bring to your mind the following possible petitions:
>
> 1. That the Institute may be kept true to the doctrinal standards of D. L. Moody, Dr. R. A. Torrey, and Dr. James M. Gray, and that its financial needs may be met happily and in triumph.
> 2. That the Extension Department may be enlarged for the promotion of evangelism and Bible teaching throughout the land, and that the financial needs of that enlargement may be forthcoming.
> 3. That the 1935 Founder's Week Conference, February 5-8, may witness the old-time power and blessing.
> 4. For the D. L. Moody Centenary and Institute Jubilee, a two-year observance: 1936—The 50th anniversary of the Institute, that 50,000 new friends may be made that year. 1937—The 100th anniversary of the birth of D. L. Moody, that through this commemoration a new realization of the value of evangelism may come

    to the church and a new desire for world-wide revival may be aroused.

5. Pray for the Alumni around the world, that there may be a new touch of the Spirit of God upon their lives.

6. Pray for Dr. Gray, that it may please the Lord to spare him to us for many years, and that in these years he may be able to reduce to writing still more of his store of Bible knowledge, so that it can be preserved for the church.

7. Pray for me that in complete dependence on a living Lord, I may be in the Institute family merely as one who serves.[8]

This emphasis on dependence on God for the Institute's expanding opportunities set the tone for Dr. Houghton's presidency.

But—an expanding program? With the economic outlook so bleak and 1937 a year of intense labor unrest in the city? Yes. Dr. Houghton plunged immediately into an active campaign to build enthusiasm about the Institute among staff and students, and confidence in it among friends and alumni.

Long years before in advertising his abilities as an actor, Will Houghton had characterized himself as a "creator of ideas." Now Dr. Houghton needed to employ this gift to the fullest in his new responsibilities. Both the times and the position demanded unusual measures to further the work—and ability beyond mere human skill.

Serving Christ sometimes demands the ultimate in devotion. Near the end of Dr. Gray's presidency, Betty Scott chose to attend Moody because she wanted to know the Bible and learn how to win souls to Christ. Her mother wrote:

> The course at Moody's gave her great spiritual poise, and the prison and street meetings, which her sensitive spirit had dreaded, turned out to be a help, and brought her no little joy.

In December 1934, just a month after Dr. Houghton's in-auguration, Communist bandits ruthlessly beheaded John and Betty Scott Stam in Tsingteh, China.

Training such students was the heart of the Moody Bible Institute. An editorial in the October 1943 *Moody Monthly* said it plainly:

> Never forget that far more significant than peace confer-ences and postwar plans, and attempted moral reform, is the sending forth of a stream of consecrated youth, to carry the gospel.

The same editorial reemphasized the Institute's tuition-free training, its emphasis on high-quality, Bible-centered educa-tion, and on practical Christian work.

But it also carried a note reminiscent of the statement in the 1895 catalog, which had said, "Great emphasis is laid upon the development and deepening of the spiritual life of the student." If this were not accomplished, then the Institute "would have failed in his case at the most important point." This dimension went beyond academics and was the dimen-sion insisted on through all the years. The *Moody Monthly* editorial concluded:

> While it is vital and essential to hold rigidly to the faith once for all delivered, this faith is to be held not only in doctrine, but in character and life.

The Institute stood, in Dr. Houghton's words, for "dis-cipline as well as doctrine." Sometimes this meant the dismis-sal of a student who consistently refused to conform to rules. This was always a traumatic experience for everyone con-cerned, and such decisions were reached only after other efforts failed.

In spite of depression and war, students came, though for a time there were many more women than men. Many of them learned lessons in trusting God they might otherwise not have learned. It was not just a matter of trusting God for money to pay bills, important as that was. Like Betty Scott, many of them had never talked to a person about Christ, or taught a class of children, or led a service in a jail chapel. They learned by experience the truth of 2 Timothy 1:7: "God hath not given us the spirit of fear; but of power, and of love, and of a sound mind," as they put classroom knowledge into practice in the laboratory of Chicago.

They also needed help to cope with the twelve or thirteen weekly one-hour required subjects. Classes were large, and students furiously scribbled copious notes trying to keep up with the lectures.

Caps and gowns were worn for the first time in the April 1936 graduation, adding to the dignity of the event. College was an impossible dream to many young people in the depression years. Many eager high school graduates wasted talents in routine jobs or drifted aimlessly because they had no money for college. Though many Institute students scraped to get money for room and board expenses, they recognized their privilege in having tuition-free training.

As Dr. Houghton once said, at Moody "pranks and prayers are in proper proportion," and there was fun as well as work. The student newspaper, first published in October 1935, reflected all the facets of Institute life.

Dr. Gray's leadership had so established the day and evening school curriculum, that Dr. Houghton could turn his gifts to promoting the school and its related ministries.

In his exciting plans, Dr. Houghton included a great evangelistic emphasis for 1936-37 to commemorate the fiftieth anniversary of the Institute and the centennial of Mr. Moody's birth. Human failure showed everywhere one looked—in money, in war, in moral standards. What better time to blazon the eternal purpose of God in human affairs. Man failed—God never did.

The Institute pushed plans to observe the two events in this country and in Great Britain, the scene of Moody's greatest evangelistic campaigns. Well-known men spoke at rallies held in many cities across the country during that year. Churches in every state in the union and in thirty foreign countries observed "Moody Day" on Sunday, February 7, 1937. Twelve thousand crowded the Chicago Coliseum on February 5, Moody's birth date, to pay tribute to him. Secular magazines and newspapers as well as Christian publications rehearsed his life and work, and honored the man whose life had honored God.

But Dr. Houghton planned expansion in other ways also. Though building slowed in the city generally, at the Institute an important building project went on. From 1937 to 1939 the new twelve-story Administration Building at 820 North LaSalle grew. The policy still held that new buildings were not erected unless the money for them was available. But friends who were eager to see the work prosper gave. One result of the D. L. Moody Centenary was a campaign to raise money for such a building to centralize the offices that were scattered in half a dozen buildings over a whole city block.

Bulldozers demolished old buildings, and the cornerstone of the new building was laid in May 1938. Three thousand people filled LaSalle Street which had been blocked to traffic for the event. At the same time work began on the basement section of the Torrey-Gray Auditorium, and both buildings were dedicated during the 1939 Founder's Week conference. The almost fifteen inches of snow on the Monday morning of the conference did not stop the crowds who came.

The Administration Building did not receive its official name, Crowell Hall, until after the death of the modest man who had been such an integral part of the Institute from the beginning of the century. Though Mr. Crowell gave a large part of the money for the building, he refused to let it be named for him.

And after all, contributions came also from the sacrificial

giving of the many across the country who believed in the
Moody Bible Institute. This itself was a testimony to Mr.
Crowell's conviction that the Institute's survival depended on
the support of many Christians.

Mr. Moody's school built and expanded in other ways than
in brick and stone during the lean depression years. Onlook-
ers and some secular historians insist that fundamentalism was
in retreat during these years and that it turned off rank and
file churchgoers. They claim that evangelical Christians were
obscurantists with a behind-the-times theology. The Moody
Bible Institute, vigorous from its beginning, laughed at the
charges. It continued its innovative thrust in education and
in literature.

And the exploding radio opportunities continued under
Dr. Houghton. The years from 1926 were an exciting, chaotic
period of expansion in radio all through the country. H. C.
Crowell's contacts with officials in Washington aided both
Dr. Gray and Dr. Houghton to iron out the complicated rela-
tionships with the government and with other radio stations.
WMBI received a good rating from a routine check by a representative of the Federal Communications Commission, which
came into being in 1934. The rating was partly due to the
care the station took in its programming to avoid offending
listeners by financial appeals or by criticizing other religious
viewpoints.

The most exciting development in these years came in 1941,
when WMBI broadcast a full day's schedule without sharing
time with any other Chicago station. WMBI went on at sun-
rise and off at sunset. The AM broadcasting day stretched
from nine hours during the winter months to fourteen and a
half during the long summer months.

Before this, WMBI was selective in its programming, using
its time wisely to meet the spiritual needs of its listeners and
to promote the school. Now with a whole day to use, the
schedule was broadened to include cultural and educational

programs, some admittedly "bait" to catch listener attention.
People tuned in to hear the news and double-checked what
they saw out the window by WMBI's weather reports.

Favorite programs continued, and new ones were added.
Aunt Theresa's KYB club brought children in every Sunday
afternoon for a quick rehearsal before program time. Parents
and children rushed from church services in the city and suburbs, eating cold lunches in cars to get to the station on time.

"Stories of Great Christians" and "Number 9 Elm Street"
brought characters to life in many kitchens and living rooms.
Housewives waited for the "Woman's Hour"; the familiar
"keep looking up," that signed off the "Shut-in Hour" closed
a program of hope and comfort.

The smooth blending of the voices of the "Announcers'
Trio" was sometimes lost in the many that joined from kitchens, hospitals, and jails to sing familiar Gospel songs.

Radio personnel lived hectic, exciting days preparing live
programs and ingeniously inventing their own sound effects
for horse's hoofs on hard streets, rain beating against a window, fire crackling in the fireplace, a lonesome train whistle
in the night. Staff members had to be constantly alert to make
right decisions, to come on the air at the right cue, or to stretch
a program to fill the allotted time. So many details must be
checked, from using copyrighted material over the air to de-
ciding whether foreign language broadcasts created clannish-
ness instead of helping to Americanize immigrants.

The depression reduced the full-time staff to four. Paid
announcements were the bread and butter of commercial stations, and at this time WMBI was not even letting listeners
know there was a financial need.

There were dreams of a brand new radio building some day,
but in the meantime the space pressure eased when the radio
staff moved to the top three floors of the new Administration
Building in 1939. Coming from its former one-room studio
crowded with piano, mikes, and chairs, its walls heavily

draped to absorb extra sounds, the staff luxuriated in its five studios, control rooms, staff offices, and visitors' galleries.

Next came application for FM, so the station could broadcast beyond the limits of the sun. Loud rejoicing greeted the Federal Communications Commission's permission to build an FM station at Addison, Illinois. A hole was dug for the foundation, but it remained a hole for two years. War restrictions froze the radio industry in the country in 1941, and no materials could be used to erect new stations or even make alterations on existing facilities.

During the war all broadcasting stations exerted extreme caution in what went out over the airwaves. The war restrictions even affected giving weather reports for fear the information might be useful to the enemy.

Restrictions on building were lifted in 1943, and in October when WMBI signed off the air at sunset, the FM station continued to send out the good news of the Gospel until nine in the evening. This FM station had the call letters WDLM, standing for—of course—Dwight Lyman Moody.

Some radio stations closed during the thirties and forties; others were denied permission to operate. But MBI's station grew to thriving maturity, partly due to the wise policies it consistently followed. Observing government regulations strictly, complete honesty in all its dealings, financial accountability, and courteous treatment of others, paid off.

No paid commercials interrupted programs, no off-color jokes or racial slurs, no cigarette or liquor ads, no frantic appeals for money are aired over WMBI. The station broadcasts programs that are in keeping with the words inscribed on the cornerstone of the transmitter building, "This is the station dedicated wholly to the service of our Lord and Saviour Jesus Christ."

Dr. Houghton used the radio in the national crisis as war burst over Europe. The country's problems in 1938 and 1939 burdened him. He wrestled with the conviction that the Institute should be a leader in the crisis days. The result was a chain broadcast called, "Let's Go Back to the Bible." Dr. Houghton announced the purpose:

> The spiritual condition of America is deplorable, indeed. Class and race hatred are being deliberately cultivated. Forces are at work spanning the spark of discontent. Conscience has gone into an eclipse, and moral standards have been thrown on the scrap heap. And in the midst of it all, the church seems quite impotent. Faith is feeble and the pulpit is dealing in platitudes. Nowhere is there a voice calling the people to repentance. Yet God has a stake in the nation and He is concerned that His word of warning and invitation shall be given forth. Extraordinary days call for extraordinary methods, and the time has come to carry our message to the people who will not seek a message. The radio is the one means of getting a hearing where the hearing is needed. It takes them unawares and lures them to listen. Every loyal Christian broadcast should be encouraged in these desperate times.
>
> Each thirty-minute period will bring some good music by Institute singers and a message of seventeen or eighteen minutes by the president of the Institute. The emphasis of the opening message will be, "Let's Go Back to the Bible." It has been turned out of the school, ignored in the home, discredited in the church. Oh, that men might see again what God's Word has meant in the life of America and what it will mean if our people return to it in repentance and faith.[9]

Each Sunday afternoon for twenty-six weeks during 1938 and 1939, stations in New York, Boston, Buffalo, Pittsburgh, Cincinnati, Detroit, Denver, Philadelphia, and WMBI in Chicago carried the program. Backed by prayer and coming from a heart burdened for revival, the program found response in many listeners who wrote their appreciation.

The first year's messages reached an even wider audience

when they were printed under the title of the broadcast. A member of the Institute's board of trustees sent a copy of the book to every member of the United States Congress with a personal letter urging careful reading of the book in view of the threatening world situation.

All this development in radio was exciting. But along came something else, something that would have delighted Mr. Moody—the Moody Institute of Science.

This part of the work began in the practical dreams of Irwin A. Moon, a young minister with a family of growing children, who was eager to reach the young people of his church. Schools and magazines and books pushed evolution, brainwashing people into accepting mere theory. He decided to show his congregation that the wonders of creation were not the result of millenniums of evolution, but the direct working of God's creative Hand. So he filmed simple scientific demonstrations to illustrate his sermons. The immediate and enthusiastic response prompted Moon to resign his church to give full time to this new calling. People jammed college and civic auditoriums to see and hear his "sermons from science" demonstrations.

Here he and Dr. Houghton crossed paths. Dr. Houghton invited Moon to join the Extension staff of the Institute with this new evangelistic-educational approach to the Gospel. He was in great demand at the San Francisco World's Fair in 1939, giving demonstrations from three to eight times a day, every day of the week.

The bombing of Pearl Harbor sent the United States into war and opened a new field to Moon. He spent the rest of the war years traveling to and from military bases, giving live demonstrations to servicemen. His free and easy style and gift of repartee made him popular with the men. Salvation emphasis was the primary purpose of his ministry always, not just demonstrating the truth of Scripture, important as that was.

His experience on the military bases proved to Moon the value of the teaching-by-film method that secular educators were experimenting with. Live demonstrations were effective but limited. He could do only one demonstration at a time. And even if he gave one, or five, or ten, every night in the year he still couldn't reach enough people. But if he could *film* the demonstrations— And so Moon's fertile mind planned.

And while he planned, he experimented. Using his home as a laboratory and his bedroom as a photographic studio, he developed a breathtaking time-lapse sequence of a flower growing and blooming.

Here Moon teamed with F. Alton Everest, formerly a professor of electrical engineering at Oregon State University. The gap which existed between evangelical Christians and knowledge of the scientific world bothered both men. They saw that so-called scientific facts, many of them mere theories, needlessly undermined confidence in the Bible. On the other hand, they knew Christians sometimes opposed true scientific discoveries out of ignorance and the fear that science *might* prove the Bible inaccurate. Moon and Everest wanted to show that God's laws were the basis of the universe and that true science supported these laws.

They wanted the Moody Bible Institute to begin a Christian laboratory. Out of this idea grew the Moody Institute of Science. The board of trustees approved the new venture which was incorporated in February 1946. Its main purpose was producing films, although live demonstrations of Sermons from Science continued.

The first film, *The God of Creation,* released during Dr. Houghton's last active year as president, received rave notices in both Christian and secular reviews. Moon's spectacular time-lapse photography portrayed many facets of creation in accurate detail. Beyond that, it accomplished its purpose of showing that creation was not just a coincidence or the result of chance evolution, but the plan of God, who had a personal interest in His creation.

The next chapter in the Moody story seems to have little connection with the Bible school idea. The school existed to train people to reach people. To reach them one had to go where they were, and sometimes this was very difficult.

This was Paul Robinson's thinking as he headed for the mission field after graduating from the Institute. He had read of the long, dangerous treks missionaries took to get to remote outposts, of their going without needed food or medicine when months-long delays kept supplies from getting in, of the death of those who could not get out to a doctor in time. So he decided to learn to fly an airplane to make his work more effective.

Pearl Harbor grounded all civilian pilots before he could get to the mission field, and by the time the war ended, his age and family responsibilities made mission boards refuse to send him out.

So he shifted his emphasis. He decided the next best thing was to pour his knowledge and enthusiasm into other young men and help them reach his dream. The idea was simply to teach potential missionaries to fly, to "use an airplane like a jeep to get around in."

When the plan was broached to the Institute board of trustees, they had to look by faith down through the long years to see its potential results. Missionary aviation was a new thing, and there were questions and qualms in the minds of many. In April 1946, the Institute leased ground at the Elmhurst, Illinois, airport not far from Chicago.

MBI's Missionary Technical Course began in this small way but soon developed into a program that trained highly skilled missionary pilots and mechanics. That story belongs in the next era of growth.

While these new visions became realities, the old, familiar ones continued to carry the Institute's imprint. The *Moody*

Bible Institute Monthly became simply the *Moody Monthly*. It added a new page directed toward young people, which gradually grew into a regular youth department called the *Youth Supplement,* a magazine within a magazine.

The number of paid subscriptions increased rapidly as prosperity returned to the country after the war. But another reason for the magazine's popularity was its continued policy of speaking out on the issues of the day and presenting the ageless remedy to current problems.

Changes were taking place in the literature outreach of the Institute. The colporteurs still went out, and books were printed and sold. But these years were difficult because people usually chose to buy bread or shoes instead of books when there was not enough money for both.

So these years were used to strengthen the work internally. Since its beginning in 1894, the BICA had been a separate organization from the Institute, with its own offices and board of directors. A. F. Gaylord and William Norton were two of the key men who carried the continuity of the Colportage Association from its first days through Dr. Houghton's presidency. Most people thought this "publishing arm of the Institute" already belonged to the organization, so in 1941 it officially became so.

But along with the union came a change as the BICA separated into two departments. The printing and sales division was called Moody Press, and its activity boomed after the depression and war years.

The missionary literature work, first called the Colportage Department, continued to distribute literature free of charge around the world. Statistics are cold figures—16,665,000 colportage books, 205,000,000 gospel leaflets. They remain cold figures unless translated into people—students, prisoners, soldiers, hospital patients, school children—all reached with Christian literature.

This tremendous literature growth came later as prosperity returned, freeing money that had been guarded for necessities.

While Dr. Houghton and his staff and the trustees searched for ways to continually reach out with new methods, the Moody Bible Institute had grown into a complex structure.

Mr. Moody's original vision had been a school. Then he reached out with an extension ministry and literature. After that came the evening school, the correspondence school, and the magazine. Now there were radio stations and the Moody Institute of Science. Behind all that was an Investment and Legal Department, a Bureau of Promotion, and a Personnel Department.

This large a work needed a good, hard look at its structure to spot any weaknesses. The board of trustees hired a professional management group to advise on correct administration and the wise use of staff, buildings, and finances. The group's comprehensive study recommended a new organizational plan.

The report praised Mr. Moody's clear vision and the able way succeeding leaders had protected the original purpose of the school. The Institute's strength lay in the way it had through the years remained true to its original purpose, maintained its doctrinal position, kept the strong loyalty of staff and students, employed a good public relations policy, enjoyed the financial support of friends.

But potential dangers lay ahead. Salaries had to be raised to give employees an adequate living standard. This meant more donors must be found, but they had to be people who believed in the work. The challenges of school, radio, publishing house, and magazine made a strong overall structure imperative.

So a reorganization established the "branch plan," with a vice-president in charge of each branch of the work, all of whom consulted regularly with the president. The executive committee had proved its value through the years and was retained. The board of trustees controlled and managed the Institute's property, funds, and all its other affairs.

This study and the changes it brought began under Dr. Houghton's leadership, but he did not live to work out the details. For years, severe migraine headaches had drained him physically and emotionally. Then in June 1946, he was rushed to the hospital with a coronary attack. Though he had a temporary recovery, he was unable to actively carry the heavy duties of his office.

For a time he kept in close touch with the work through the dean of education, but eventually even this became impossible. Dr. Houghton died in June 1947.

Dr. H. A. Ironside and Dr. William Culbertson conducted the funeral service at Moody Memorial Church. In his message of tribute, Dr. Culbertson quoted one of Dr. Houghton's songs which summed his entire life's purpose. It was the poem he had written in memory of John and Betty Stam.

> Help me to know the value of these hours,
>   Help me the folly of all waste to see;
> Help me to trust the Christ who bore my sorrows,
>   And thus to yield for life or death to Thee.
> In all my ways be glorified, Lord Jesus,
>   In all my ways guide me with Thine own eye;
> Just when and as Thou wilt, use me, Lord Jesus,
>   And then for me 'tis Christ, to live or die.*

Sixty years earlier Mr. Moody had exclaimed, "We need a school to teach men and women the Bible and how to use it to win people to Christ." His successors had built and protected the school through two world wars, shattered moral standards, and a severe depression. All the way along, winning people to Christ had been the heartbeat of the work. That was the reason for its existence.

*Words by Will Houghton. Copyright 1938, renewed 1959, by the Rodeheaver Company, Winona Lake, Indiana 46590. Used by permission.

Dr. Houghton summed it all in his song, "Lead Me to Some Soul Today," written in memory of Mr. Moody.

> Lead me to some soul today,
>   O teach me, Lord, just what to say;
> Friends of mine are lost in sin,
>   And cannot find their way.
> Few there are who seem to care,
>   And few there are who pray;
> Melt my heart and fill my life,
>   Give me one soul today.†

†Words by Will Houghton. Copyright 1936, renewed 1964, by the Hope Publishing Co., Carol Stream, Illinois 60187. Used by permission.

"YOUNG MAN, how would you like to multiply your life a thousand times over?" The question was direct, challenging.

The young pastor listened, but thought, *Can't I do that just as well as a pastor?*

But the question would not go away. Teaching in a Bible school did open wider doors than pastoring a church. It meant preparing many pastors for many churches. It *was* a multiplication.

Then young William Culbertson remembered the words of a seminary professor: "I want to remember every day that my body is a temple of the Holy Spirit, because it makes a difference in the way I live."

Could *he* live a godly life? If so, then its multiplication would be valuable in God's service.

5

William Culbertson: Multiplying a Vision

WORLD WAR II shattered Europe, leaving many of its magnificent, historic buildings in rubble, its economy in ruin, its young men in graves, its people in despair. Years of rebuilding lay ahead, some of it never to be completed.

But the United States emerged, shining and untarnished. The war ended the depression and began the age of affluence. The shortage of civilian goods because of the depression first and then the all-out war effort had made people *things* hungry. The industrial expansion of the 1940s and 1950s barely kept pace with the demands for the necessities that a few short years before had been luxuries.

In all this Americans were not selfish. Europe's devastation made massive American aid imperative to stave off its complete collapse. The Marshall Plan, churches, and private groups all joined in the relief effort.

President Harry Truman did not face the rigid opposition Woodrow Wilson did when he proposed the League of Nations. The strong isolationist mood after the first war did not develop after World War II. The Senate quickly approved the United States entrance into the United Nations.

Instead of the organization bringing a stable peace in the world, increasing tensions marred the troubled forties. The Cold War between the United States and the Soviet Union, the Berlin blockade, conflict in China, all encouraged the

United States and western European nations to form the NATO Alliance for mutual aid.

The extent of the atrocities against Jews horrified the world as emaciated figures stumbled through the opened gates of German concentration camps. As a result the sympathy of much of the world supported the birth of the State of Israel in 1948.

On the other side of the world, Communist China's threat loomed, raising the specter of totalitarianism again. This fear of Communism sparked the shameful McCarthy era of suspicion in the early 1950s. And the country was scarcely out of World War II when the Korean War drafted young men again in June of 1950. War machinery threatened in every country.

Economic experts warned that the early 1950s would be critical years in the world's history. In spite of affluence, people were jittery.

In 1954 the words "under God" were added to the Pledge of Allegiance, and that same year the Supreme Court outlawed segregation in public schools. However, federal troops had to be called out in Little Rock, Arkansas, in 1957-58 to enforce the decision when the governor of the state himself barred the school doorway against black children.

Unease grew in the world with the Soviet Union's 1957 electrifying announcement of the first successful orbit of the satellite, Sputnik I. Americans felt the unease the most; somehow they had been left behind. This triggered a Russia-United States race to the moon which cost the United States billions in dollars and the lives of three astronauts. Science and technology and math became the chief emphasis in education, while literature and history took a backseat. And then millions watched Neil Armstrong take that first "one small step" on the moon in 1969.

During John F. Kennedy's term as president, the Bay of Pigs fiasco, the erection of the Berlin Wall which made East

Germany a prison, and the Cuban missile crisis paralyzed the world with suspicion and fear.

The sixties proved to be a tragic decade as assassins gunned down first President Kennedy, then Martin Luther King, and then Robert Kennedy. These senseless tragedies were only the tip of the iceberg of turmoil that shifted in a divisive spirit across the nation. President Johnson escalated the Vietnam War in 1965 and sparked a violent anti-war movement which spread out in many directions and swept up a protesting tide of followers.

Opposition to the 1964 sweeping Civil Rights Act exploded in riots in many cities, one of the most destructive and frightening taking place in the Watts area of Los Angeles. This restless protest spawned a variety of issues: demands for black power and students' rights, marches for ecology, counterculture advocates, women's liberation, an alarming rise in drug use, the rock music craze, and a general alienation of youth who demanded freedom from all restraint and authority. People glibly used terms like "new morality," "population explosion," "death of God," and "post-Christian era."

The 1920s had been marked by jazz and bathtub gin; the 1930s by fear and poverty. The 1960s had its distinctives also. One of the most prominent was the surging interest in mysticism, astrology, the occult, and eastern religions. LSD and other drugs were hailed as substitutes for a religious experience.

A variety of religious moods swept people back and forth. An emphasis on having faith in faith and talk of the power of positive thinking gained vast followers through books by Norman Vincent Peale, Fulton J. Sheen, and Anne Morrow Lindbergh. Existentialism intrigued many with its revolt against absolutes, particularly—as in all ages—against the absolutes of Scripture.

But all the news was not doubt and confrontation and protest. The late forties and fifties brought revival in a measure among young people. Inter-Varsity Christian Fellowship actively promoted Bible study on campuses. Billy Graham's influence grew phenomenally from 1949 into the 1960s. Campus Crusade for Christ reached collegians with its *Four Spiritual Laws* and emphasis on sharing Christ, as did the Navigators with their strong Scripture memory program.

The Dead Sea Scrolls discoveries in caves in Jordan, especially the famous Isaiah scroll, witnessed the validity of Scripture to those who needed such confirmation.

Another outgrowth of the sixties was the Jesus movement with its varying depths of experience, some genuine and some superficial.

Much that took place in these years throughout the nation was true in capsule form in the city of Chicago. The soldiers received a tumultuous parade down Michigan Avenue, and then could not find jobs to make a living. Fortunately the GI Bill opened college doors to many.

The energy and vitality of the city's people and business were seen in its population growth, its increased retail trade, and its new buildings. Urban development beautified many sections of the city. The Chicago Plan Commission approved a Model Cities program which bulldozed slums and relocated people in huge housing projects. Unfortunately they in turn often became slums. The Chicago Circle Campus, a commuter school, resulted from such an urban renewal project. Headstart and Operation Push attempted to give help to the poor and hopeless as the old settlement houses had done during Moody's day.

In 1955 the Prudential Building went up, the first new office building since 1934. Among other items in its cornerstone was a map showing the number of former Moody students and their location on mission fields. That same year Richard J. Daley was elected to his first term as mayor of the city. A gigantic filtration plant dedicated in 1966 assured the city of pure water.

In 1967 the city's normal frantic pace stopped for several days when a massive snow storm temporarily halted life. Institute students built snowmen in the middle of usually traffic-crowded LaSalle Street.

Ghetto blacks had expressed their frustration periodically since that bad incident in 1919. But those outbreaks were nothing compared to the wild anger that boiled over in the city in 1968 with Martin Luther King's assassination. The violence, looting, and burning was especially bad on Chicago's West Side.

Later that summer the Democratic National Convention plastered a never-to-be-forgotten image of Chicago across television screens from coast to coast. Millions watched demonstrators and police battle in the streets and parks with sticks and stones and obscenities. The next year the Weathermen faction of the Students for a Democratic Society went on a window-breaking spree in the Loop to vent their so-called days of rage.

Regardless of the events in the world, and no matter what happened in the city, cars congested expressways bringing people in to work from the suburbs and then taking them away again at the close of the day. The commotion of the daytime city became an echo in the deserted night streets, making people afraid to walk alone.

Many of these events were still future when Dr. William Culbertson stepped across from the dean of education office to the presidency.

He was born in 1905 in Philadelphia, and accepted Jesus Christ as his Saviour when he was nine years old. This was not surprising; he was a serious-minded boy, raised in a godly home.

He felt God's call to the ministry, and when he graduated

from high school he was able to enroll immediately in the Reformed Episcopal Seminary in Philadelphia. Many great servants of God preached in Philadelphia during those years and deeply impressed the young seminary student with the importance of the Word of God, an importance he later stressed many times as president of Moody Bible Institute.

In 1929 he married Catharine Gantz, the girl he had proposed to four years earlier. She was a strong helper, providing a homelife that was his refuge and backing his ministry with prayer. She did more; her quick wit and humor balanced his serious nature. Their two sons and two daughters enriched their lives.

The Culbertson family battled the depression along with millions of other Americans. One church issuing him a call frankly said it could not pay him a regular salary or provide housing. This did not keep the young pastor, his wife, and two little children from accepting the call. The years were crammed full of activity as William Culbertson pastored, taught at both the Reformed Episcopal Seminary and the Philadelphia School of Bible, completed his college education, and received the doctor of divinity degree from his seminary.

Dr. Culbertson and Dr. Gray had much in common. They were both members of the Reformed Episcopal Church, and both were scholarly, well educated men. Elected as a bishop in his denomination, Dr. Culbertson supervised churches in eastern New York and Pennsylvania, New Jersey, Maryland, and Delaware. This meant visiting the churches on a regular yearly basis and giving spiritual counsel to pastors. In these contacts one fact became clear. Christians had to translate doctrinal belief into living faith if they were to reach the man on the street. But this was possible only if belief had the right foundation.

Like Dr. Gray, William Culbertson had an unshakeable conviction of the absolute dependability of Scripture. As pas-

tor and educator at this time of open scorn for those who ad-
hered to the Word, his allegiance to the Bible never wavered.

Mr. Moody once said he could not have fellowship with
those who denied the deity of Christ. Dr. Culbertson felt as
strongly about those who denied the faith. He flatly refused to
join those Christians who criticized fellow believers for every
little difference in viewpoint, but he reserved his judgment
for those who claimed to be Christians yet did not accept the
"supremacy of God's Living Word and God's Written Word."

This strong conviction kept him from supporting the National Council of Churches and the World Council of
Churches, believing they represented a "unity of disbelief."
He refused to "be associated in an ecumenical movement that
includes those who deny [Christ]."

At various times while he was in Philadelphia, Dr. Houghton heard Dr. Culbertson preach and invited him to speak at
the 1939 Founder's Week Conference. Dr. Houghton was
convinced that the times demanded strong, vigorous, well-
trained students; and that these came only from strong, vigorous, gifted teachers. He saw this teaching gift in Dr. Culbertson and invited him to join the Institute faculty.

The Culbertsons, burdened by issues in the denomination,
did not feel they could leave their church just then. But finally
in 1942, they moved to a quiet, residential street in Evanston,
and Dr. Culbertson plunged into active work as the dean of
education. *Newsweek* magazine carried the announcement of
his coming, calling him a "large, plain, and cheerful man."

God's timing brought Dr. Culbertson to the Institute to fit
him into the organization, familiarize him with administrative details, and endear him to students and staff at just the
right time. During 1946, when Dr. Houghton was desperately
ill and away from his office, Dr. Culbertson handled his work
and the president's. He filled in as acting president for a year
after Dr. Houghton's death. Then in February 1948, the board
of trustees elected him president. Students and employees

stood to greet the announcement with applause and the singing of the Doxology.

Dr. Houghton, the "creator of ideas," was a difficult man to follow. No one was more conscious of the differences in their abilities and personalities than Dr. Culbertson. But as Dr. Houghton's gifts were right for his time, so Dr. Culbertson's were for his. He had the wisdom and patience that the events of his administration demanded.

No other era covered the wild extremes of this one he faced. It ranged from the relative quiet of the Eisenhower years through the wild protest and revolutionary lifestyles of the 1960s. Dr. Culbertson met theological doubts, questions about prophecy, attacks against the Scripture, extremes in dress and conduct. Through it all he represented the Institute's stability.

A 1966 Founder's Week message expressed his stand through those years:

> As president of the Moody Bible Institute, I want to sound again the word of warning. If we as orthodox, as Evangelicals, as fundamentalists move from this doctrine [the inspiration of the Word of God] we are doomed to disaster.

His quiet, deliberate waiting on God for His leading in each situation became the stabilizing force of the Institute during the turbulent period. Controversial discussions in faculty or other meetings never got him excited. He was concerned, but he never shouted down opposition. When students came with complaints and suggestions for change, he listened patiently.

Tempers frayed easily because the situation often was bleak. Funds had been so low during the depression years that salaries had not kept pace with rising living costs. Employees lacked an adequate retirement and pension plan. Anxiety over the pressures of living lowered Institute morale and a spirit of defeatism brought criticism and faultfinding.

The solution was twofold: the administration must share

more of the problems it faced, and it must be more considerate of employees and understanding of their problems. And through it all was the reminder, "Isn't it wonderful that in our need we have God?"

As dean of education and then as president, Dr. Culbertson thought through the school's entrance requirements. The 1943-44 catalog still listed the range of its purpose from those called of God to full-time service to those just wanting to study the Bible to better serve Christ in their local church. This was Moody's original purpose preserved through the years. With this wide a category of students, educational requirements could not be rigid. But changes in other schools' academic standards could not be ignored. So high school graduation was required for all who enrolled.

Another problem was the age barrier of twenty as the minimum. The Institute lost young people who were impatient to get into college right from high school. So in 1949 the age limit went down to eighteen.

After the war, college enrollments nationwide zoomed as the GI Bill sent many to college who could not go otherwise or whose college career had been interrupted by the war. The Institute wanted its share of these eager young people, but it faced what seemed at that time an insurmountable problem of insufficient dormitory and classroom space. Music students waited in line for practice rooms.

Worse still was the deteriorating neighborhood. The area bordering the school had not yet come under urban renewal. It was not safe even to walk LaSalle Street within sight of the dorms, and the girls housed several blocks from the main campus were in constant potential danger. Those on ground floors did not feel safe even with bars at the windows. There was clamor by students, parents, and donors to move to a safer neighborhood, perhaps even out of the city to a campus of grass and trees.

The decision was difficult, but after long discussion and

prayer, the board of trustees voted to remain on LaSalle Street. Too much money was invested in the existing property and buildings to make a change. And, anyway, the school had been designed for location in an area that gave practical as well as book learning. The mission field of Chicago had proved its importance to the Institute over and over again. Moody students, "beggars who had the bread of life," had an obligation to share with Chicagoans.

Staying in the city meant the problems had to be solved. Postwar prosperity slowly began to bring more money to buy property and to tear down many of the neighboring old builddings to make way for new. The city of Chicago confirmed the trustees' decision by vacating Institute Place and selling the whole block to Moody. From 1950 to 1969 the Institute busily carried on its own renewal program. Gradually a beautiful open campus began to emerge in the heart of the city of concrete and steel.

The first building, the most essential at that time, was ten-story Houghton Hall, a women's dormitory, built on the historic Chicago and LaSalle corner where once the Chicago Avenue Church had stood. Classes that fall of 1950 suffered through the noisy pounding of piles driven deep for foundations. Tunnels connected the Institute buildings so that students dashed to classes or meals without stopping for coats.

Houghton Hall was an expansion "remarkable in an era when war and change might be expected to weaken orthodox religion's appeal to an embittered and skeptical humanity," wrote the *Chicago Daily News* in November 1951.

In addition to this new building, old ones which had lined Chicago Avenue and Wells Street for many years came down, and space opened for future building. In 1955 the Torrey-Gray Auditorium and the Doane Memorial Music Building were dedicated. A much-needed academic building went up in 1960-61, appropriately named for Dr. P. B. Fitzwater, a forty-year member of faculty. The four-story building housed classrooms, faculty offices, the Missionary Radio Technology Department, and the audio-visual center.

Dr. Fitzwater could not even dream of the facilities available to faculty in the building named for him. They included standard chalkboards and maps, which were not always available when the first classes met. But the audiovisual center goes far beyond with tape-recording lines for each classroom, closed circuit and off-the-air television facilities, an intercommunication system, and a language laboratory. All are designed to make better teachers and learners.

Finally in 1967 a much-needed men's dormitory was begun. Its twenty stories house all the single men students and the offices of the dean of students' department. It was named and dedicated in honor of Dr. Culbertson, over his vigorous protests.

While approving the changes, some returning alumni had secret regrets, because the entire interior of the familiar block vanished. The original 153 Building, Institute Place buildings, the Sweet Shop, the old Guild House, the old iron railing fell into the jaws of the giant bulldozers. The entire area was opened and beautified with brick and concrete pavement interspersed with grass-covered circles. The Alumni Plaza gives a feeling of space to the campus, and an aura of quiet in the commotion of the concrete city surrounding it.

Some things are different; frisbees fly on warm spring evenings. But some things remain the same; laughter still drifts across the campus as it did when the old buildings hemmed the students.

Accompanying these changes, a beautiful new student dining room opened, the envy of food service people from other college-level schools. And with the favorite Sweet Shop gone, a new, employee Coffee Cove opened in the basement of Crowell Hall.

At this time a building in the block just north of the main campus became available to the Institute. Originally a Masonic Lodge, extensive renovation made it useable as a gymnasium. Upper floors have facilities for the Married Women's Guild and the student newspaper and yearbook offices.

During this transformation of the Chicago campus, vital parts of the Institute farther away also improved their facilities.

The school's Wood Dale Airport, once adequate for the flight training program, had only an uncomfortable two miles separating it from Chicago's O'Hare airport, the busiest airport in the world, by this time. The flight school needed a location that would simulate mission field conditions of more mountainous terrain, climate differences, and water for float training. Officials found it in Elizabethton, Tennessee, a small town in the foothills of the Great Smokey Mountains that was green in summer, red-gold in autumn.

The staff designed the aviation campus in Elizabethton since they knew just what their specialty training required. The result was a building that housed a big maintenance hangar, shops, classrooms, instructor's offices, and a lounge surrounded by windows that let in the beauty of the outside world.

This beautiful Henry Coleman Crowell Building was dedicated in April 1970, in memory of the man whose enthusiasm had pushed the aviation dream into reality.

In the meantime, the Moody Institute of Science found a building adequate for its needs in Whittier, California. The trustees bought property for bookstores in other parts of Chicago and for radio stations in other cities.

How could all this go on when back at the main campus officials were on their knees asking God for money for the day to day operating expenses? The answer lies in the policy the Institute follows of using money as the contributor requests. If money comes in designated specifically for a new building, the request is honored, even though there might be a pressing need in another area of the work.

The buildings were essential because the work was growing. As it grew, constant checking kept the school fixed to the uniqueness of its original purpose. This meant administration and faculty had to be alert to educational trends. Would developments in secular education fit Moody's purpose? Sometimes the answer was yes, sometimes no.

By 1951 the school's schedule was obviously outdated. When Moody began in 1886, classes met the year round, and it did not matter when a student enrolled because eventually he caught up with the whole cycle. Then for many years the Institute operated on a three-term per year plan which graduated students in April, August, and December. This left only one free month, giving students no chance to earn money for the next year's expenses. Also, this schedule was out of line with other schools, making it difficult for a student to transfer into Moody or out of Moody to fit the cycle of another school.

So the Institute moved to the semester plan, changing its courses from two eleven-month years to three two-semester years. The advantages of the change were clear: Students were free to take summer jobs or put their training into practice in camps or in their home churches; they could more easily transfer into or out of other schools; ninety-six semester hour courses made it possible for the Institute to receive college accreditation; a six-week summer school attracted people not regularly enrolled and kept the facilities from lying idle. And it gave time before the busy fall for maintenance people to repaint and repair so that the Institute property always looked in top condition.

A two-year transition period allowed for a smooth change, so that no student's schedule was disrupted. Those who entered in 1951 under the term plan finished under it in 1953.

This semester change made necessary an extensive curriculum revision, which combined the many one-hour subjects into two, three, or four-hour courses. Seven of the courses, the General Bible, Pastors, Missionary, Christian Education,

Christian Education-Music, Music, and Jewish Missions required three years to graduate. The Missionary Technical Course took four years because students spent two years at the Chicago campus studying Bible and missionary subjects, followed by two years of intensive training at the flight school in Tennessee.

Soon after the aviation course began, it became evident that flying a plane was not for all missionaries. A very good missionary might make a very poor pilot. And not all missionaries wanted to learn to fly; some were perfectly happy to keep their feet on the ground.

The Missionary Aviation Fellowship, though cool to the every-missionary-a-pilot idea, enthusiastically supported the prospect of trained missionary technical specialists who would serve fellow missionaries.

So the Missionary Technical Course changed in 1949 "to meet the recognized need for missionaries who have technical knowledge as well as Bible Institute training." One part of the training is as important as the other, for the men are missionary pilots.

Changes came as the course developed. By 1954 two majors were offered in the Missionary Technical Course: aviation flight and mechanics, and radio and communications. The radio major trained men in point-to-point two-way radio communication on isolated mission fields. Later, a broadcast major trained them for the technical aspects of radio broadcasting.

From the very beginning of the flight program, the Institute had been wary of moving too fast and sending out men who were interested only in the glamour of flying. So the screening of those applying to the program was tightened, purposely making the program hard to get into. Too much depended on a pilot's ability to think clearly and react quickly to let just anyone graduate from the course. Candidates had to attend a week-long flight camp to determine their fitness and their aptitude for flying even before being accepted into the program.

The testing process continues throughout the entire intensive program. Each student must pass rigid government regulations as well as the high standards of Institute instructors. The men do not just learn to fly a plane. They learn to fly a plane safely under the emotional pressure of a possible emergency landing under far from ideal weather and ground conditions. Usually mission field terrain is rugged with high grass, soft fields, and sloping ground. Landing strips are often short and uneven. The training also includes the know-how of keeping a plane running mechanically. A pilot on a mission field may find himself hundreds of miles from a repair shop and must improvise spare parts.

Moody Bible Institute took a daring step in initiating this type of specialized training. The new, untried idea of a missionary flight program proved its value as it brought remote people into the world family and gave isolated missionaries the comfort of knowing that emergency help was within reach of flying minutes.

The 1962 annual report looked back at what had been accomplished:

> In the last 15 years since the regular missionary has left the mission field flying in the hands of the missionary technical specialist, not a single missionary airman nor his passengers have been lost except in the hands of hostile savages. . . . The key to this fine record lies in the highly skilled, specially trained missionary airman. Furthermore, we can now say that most of these aviators have received their training at the Moody Bible Institute and the proportion is rapidly increasing. There is no school and few other adequate sources from which specially trained personnel of this kind may be obtained. Missionary aviation, as a significant movement today, looks to Moody for its supply of manpower.

In 1961 the school was seventy-five years old. When it began, every student studied Bible, music, and how to use what they learned to reach people for Christ. Mr. Moody's, "Never mind the Greek and Hebrew" sentiment had been modified through the years as English, Christian Education, pastoral training, and Greek and Hebrew became essentials.

But by the early 1960s, pressure came to make a drastic change in the Institute's structure. Insistent voices demanded that the Institute become a Bible college and grant degrees. Degrees, they said, were the "hallmark of academic preparation." A school which did not offer a degree was considered inferior, no matter how specialized or professional the training might be.

The question remained whether this was the road the Institute should take. What *was* an institute anyway? It was not a college, but a professional school of specialized training; in Moody's case, specialized Bible training.

Through the years Dr. Culbertson had grappled with this issue and had formulated his personal philosophy of education. He stated it clearly:

> Bible institutes from the time of their origin . . . have stressed those things needed for vital Christian witness: the study of the English Bible, the winning of souls, spiritual living, missionary outreach, and gospel hymnody.
>
> While certain elements have been added to the course of study, these basics remain intact. As I see it, the Bible institute is a specialized school, distinct from the liberal arts college, from the theological seminary, and from a scientific institute. Some speak of it as a religious, undergraduate, professional school.[10]

To change to a Bible College would change the Institute's purpose.

Aware of the swirling attitudes, faculty and administration began a self-study program to determine the best way to improve the Institute's academic standards. All were committed to the belief that the Lord's service demanded those who had the highest possible intellectual and spiritual qualifications. But they intended to guard against the academic becoming more important than the spiritual.

So a detailed questionnaire went out to alumni and students, asking that they evaluate their training and give an opinion about granting degrees. The answer came back: We value our training, but we feel the Institute must give a degree.

The faculty discussed the matter thoroughly in weekly meetings—and in the Sweet Shop during coffee breaks. The options were either to maintain the status quo; go to a four-year college course; or combine the Institute course and a liberal arts course at an accredited college.

In 1965 Dr. Culbertson summarized his thinking to the faculty as he stressed the need for some kind of change. But going to a four-year college program was not the answer, for that would, in his words, "secularize the campus." It would open a Pandora's box of new problems. It would not be easy to find qualified teachers for literature, history, sociology, and psychology classes who were also strong evangelical Christians. He was no more in favor of competing with colleges and seminaries than Mr. Moody had been. Dr. Culbertson's main concern was that the distinctives of the Bible training not be lost in a surge of general education. Offering a degree program did not mean that Moody Bible Institute was becoming either a liberal arts or a Bible college.

The administration insisted that

> The uniqueness of Moody Bible Institute must be preserved. It is today subject to pressures that it change its course, that it become like thousands of other schools which surround it in our nation.[11]

From the long hours of prayer and discussion came the solution. The Institute would continue giving its regular diploma to those graduating from the three-year course. But a student who entered the Institute with two years of credit from an accredited liberal arts college would receive a bachelor's degree when he finished the Institute's three-year program. Students who went on from Moody and earned at least fifty-four hours of credit in a liberal arts college could return for an Institute degree by taking six additional hours of Bible. This formula combined a liberal arts education with Bible Institute training in a five-year preparation for Christian service.

The degree program preserved most of the Institute's historic curriculum. However, it changed the original course plan, which dated back to the founding of the school, to a system of majors, giving students more flexibility in their choice of subjects. They could earn a diploma and/or a bachelor of arts degree in either: Bible Theology, Pastoral Training, Evangelism, Church Music, Christian Education, Christian Education-Music, Foreign Missions, Communications, or Jewish and Modern Israel Studies. A bachelor of science degree was given for Missionary Technology and Missionary Nursing.

Both students and faculty knew that curriculum is only as good as those who teach it. Buildings and equipment and curriculum do not make a school. James A. Garfield's statement about a good education needing only a student at one end of a bench and a true teacher at the other still held true. Years before, Mr. Moody had built the school's reputation by inviting men to teach who were well known leaders of Christian thought and action. And succeeding years built a faculty of consecrated men and women of God who were unusually well qualified for their ministry of training through preparation and experience. Students were not interested in big names; they wanted teachers who knew their subject and cared about their students.

Spiritual depth remained the essential quality looked for

in a teacher. Without a deep commitment to Christ, a string of degrees after a person's name meant nothing. However, it could not be denied that the number of faculty-earned degrees raised the stature of a school in academic circles. So the goal was to find men and women of spiritual warmth and discernment who were academically trained, who had a teaching gift, and who agreed with the Institute's doctrinal stand on the Bible alone.

Because the day and evening schools were so closely connected, change in one affected the other, especially the 1951 move from the term plan to the semester system. Adult education boomed across the country during the years after the war.

Moody had specialized in such education since the Evening Department first began in 1903—and before that in the heyday of the Chicago Bible work back in 1873. Now it offered various levels of instruction. The two-year Basic Bible program satisfied those who needed a simpler level of instruction. The General Evening Course was more advanced and took longer to finish. If a student pushed, he could finish the course in three years by taking six subjects a week—a pretty rugged schedule for those working full-time jobs.

Other changes sharpened the evening school when the degree program went into the day school. The basic and general programs were retained so that no student would be denied opportunity for training. But a new plan gave students more flexibility in meeting graduation requirements. A thirty-six hour program gave a student a chance to complete six series of six credits each from Bible, theology, Christian education, communications, or missions. He received a special certificate when he finished each series. Earning six certificates qualified a student to graduate from evening school.

Then a Day-Evening program was added in 1967 and offered day school subjects during the evening in two- or three-hour blocks. Those who enrolled had to meet the same academic standards day school students did if they wanted credit for the course.

The variety of subjects and flexibility of the evening program brings students to crowd the classrooms. Every Monday, Tuesday, and Thursday evening housewives, pastors, mechanics, teachers, plumbers, and musicians hurry from home or work for this specialized training.

No fixed number limits those who may enroll, since students live off campus, but many factors control the attendance. Vacations, health problems, the weather, economic conditions, and even expressway traffic can cut the response. The unrest in the city of Chicago during the protests of the sixties dropped the enrollment temporarily, because people were afraid to come out on the dark city streets.

Anyone knows that evening school had a place back in 1890, and probably in 1900, and 1910. But is it still needed? In 1889 students went into the city to teach Bible classes; to visit in homes, hospitals, and jails; to give out literature; and to speak personally to people. Chicago had changed during the years; its streets improved, its buildings grew higher, its people became more sophisticated. But its need for salvation remained, and evening school students still train to meet that need.

Some Chicago churches are pastored by men whose only training came from classes at Moody Evening School. Sunday school teachers learn how to teach the Bible to answer wiggly beginners' "whys" and to challenge junior-age enthusiasms. Many housewives use material from an evening school class in teaching neighborhood Bible groups.

Continuing education is the current term for anything beyond high school, and the correspondence school's climbing enrollment shows its value. For a time around 1950, the downward business trend in the country slowed enrollment, but since then new interest has come mainly due to the restructuring of courses.

College credit courses were another development of these years. These give transfer credit into day school at Moody or into other Bible schools or colleges. Some secular colleges recognize Moody Correspondence School college credit courses as being equivalent to their religion courses and give transfer credit.

Letters pouring into the Correspondence School department tell of courses used for individual study, group study, as the curriculum in evening schools conducted by churches, and as part of the elective courses in youth and adult Sunday school classes.

The president of a school like Moody handles more than cut and dried, routine administrative details. One of Dr. Culbertson's major weekly responsibilities was the chapel message each Monday to students and employees. Sometimes he dealt with practical matters of Christian conduct; sometimes he warmed hearts from a portion of Scripture; always he challenged to godly living. He did not want students to be isolated from the world during their years of training, so he kept them aware of the issues of the day—the political strife, the race problems, the theological questions, the changes in moral standards.

All the students came to the Institute from the culture of the times. Some came from unsaved homes, some from high schools and churches with very permissive standards, others from strict backgrounds.

They came, a thousand of them, to live together day after day in one city block. And they found rules. Some rules were necessary—for safety in the city, for smooth living together. Some of the rules were questioned.

Administration and deans had to face the questions and decide which rules were really needed. Those that were simply carried on the books from several generations back were reevaluated and dropped if they no longer served a purpose.

Others were retained, even though the reasons for them could not always be explained to student satisfaction.

One of the problems Dr. Culbertson had to help iron out was how much liberty the student newspaper editors had. Students at the Institute have always been in a different situation from those in other schools because they receive tuition-free training from the gifts of Institute donors. Though grateful, some students saw this as a club the Institute wielded to keep them from expressing legitimate complaints.

The *Moody Student* began as a paper to let friends know what God was doing at the Institute, and it was largely just human interest stories. Gradually it became geared more directly to the students and expressed student opinion.

Finally the question, How much liberty does the student paper have to freely air complaints against school policy? precipitated heated debate. With views ranging from "no freedom at all," to "total freedom," a middle course was established.

The *Moody Student* should express student opinion but not air individual complaints. A temporary resentment should not be allowed to harm the Institute's total ministry. The gain to a student of blowing off steam was small compared to the possible loss to him and fellow students of the prayer and financial support of friends of the work.

But in this matter and in other issues another policy of the Institute was made clear to everyone. No basic policy of the school should be changed just to please donors. Administration, employees, and students alike were accountable to God for their words and actions and attitudes.

During the troubled sixties with student unrest the chief concern on many college campuses, it was minimal at the Institute. One graduate publicly burned his diploma in protest at alleged Institute discrimination. And some students rejoiced on graduation day that rules and regulations were forever left behind.

Dr. Culbertson wanted all the students to find answers for the questions of the times in the Word of God, and be able to "give a reason for the hope that was in them" when they graduated. They were his sons and daughters, and he wanted God's best for them.

But the president of Moody does more than direct a school because MBI is more than a school. To some, Moody Bible Institute means Moody Press. And, Moody Press itself means different things to different people. To some it's Bible study aids and Bible translations. To others it's fiction and biography and missionary books. A textbook division began in 1955 to produce books from an evangelical viewpoint on Bible study, theology, church history, archaeology, psychology, and church music.

Four Moody Bookstores in the Chicago area keep sales clerks busy. Moody Press salesmen span the country, welcomed by Christian bookstore managers who know Moody Press *is* a name they can trust. In bygone years colporteurs went out with stacks of books under their arms; now the retail catalog service ships out huge orders daily.

The tremendous growth of Moody Press out of its humble beginnings in the basement of a small frame house would have made D. L. Moody the businessman happy. But Moody would rejoice even more at the outreach of the Press in literature distribution. When the BICA became an organic part of the Institute under Dr. Houghton, the Colportage Department, later renamed Moody Literature Mission, took the responsibility of distributing literature free of charge.

Over the years MLM gave millions of dollars worth of tracts, books, and Bibles to public schools, libraries, prisons, hospitals, and city missions. In secluded mountain sections and pioneer districts where there was no church, people were saved through words printed on a page. A chaplain wrote, "Since I last received material from you, I've moved halfway around the world to this lonely spot in Korea. Now again I would like to ask you for reading material for our men. We need it."

A 1953 report estimated that that year alone twelve million people had received some piece of Christian literature from MLM.

From the very beginning the BICA sent literature overseas. In the late forties the Institute revamped its procedures, because its limited funds had to be wisely spent. Rather than sending American written and printed literature to foreign countries, the Institute gave money to print the material in the country where it was to be used. An established mission board promised to raise half the money for the project, and Moody Literature Mission matched the amount.

Other mission boards heard of the project and wanted to be a part of it. About sixty mission executives met with Moody Press and MLM leaders to see if they could unite to produce and distribute literature. The result was the Evangelical Literature Overseas whose purpose was

> To promote and encourage the writing, production, printing and distribution of Evangelical Christian literature around the world and primarily for use in foreign countries and in foreign languages . . . and to provide funds for such purposes and to assist in all ways possible the writing, translation, publishing, and distribution of such literature.[12]

This new organization was immediately besieged with pleas for help from mission organizations. Though the ELO was not a direct part of the Institute, its origin and success came through the financial help and encouragement of the Colportage Department. So Mr. Moody's eagerness to reach people with the Gospel through literature multiplied even beyond the boundaries of his vision.

Not only does MBI mean a school and a press, to some it means a magazine. Each change in the Institute's leadership resulted in some changes in *Moody Monthly's* content and layout, and this was true under Dr. Culbertson. Wilbur M. Smith's "In the Study" became a popular feature; the "Idea Notebook" gave specific help to Christian workers; "Off the Record" reviewed sacred recordings.

The magazine continued to give the dependable help in Bible study, evangelism, current issues, and religious news that readers expected from a magazine put out by the Moody Bible Institute.

Skimming articles and editorials through the 1950s and 1960s shows the way the editors faced issues of the day. And it shows too how problems recur through the years. Back in 1903 H. P. Crowell acted against the open vice in Chicago. In the 1950s a *Moody Monthly* editorial declared, "Christians *Should* Get Angry" at pornography. Today pornography is one of the gravest problems facing the nation.

To some MBI spells Moody Institute of Science. Though still in the pioneer, experimenting stage when it produced the *God of Creation,* it began to stretch and grow. During Dr. Culbertson's presidency, MIS produced eighteen science films, among them the fascinating *Dust or Destiny, Voice of the Deep, Time and Eternity, Red River of Life,* and *City of the Bees.*

Churches eagerly advertised film showings, knowing they would draw a crowd. But MIS science films had an impact in other places also. Some branches of the armed services used them as a part of their basic training of new recruits. Huge corporations such as Chrysler, General Foods, General Electric, and Eastern Airlines used them in employee meetings. By mid-1968 MIS had a hundred foreign language versions of the films so missionaries could multiply their usefulness.

People thronging the Seattle World's Fair in 1962, the New York World's Fair in 1964-65, and the Montreal Expo in 1967 heard the gospel through the films and the Sermons from Science demonstrations.

But the outreach of MIS goes beyond its well-known films.

It produced leadership training materials and Bible teaching aids. Then it moved into educational science films for public schools. These films have a moral rather than a spiritual ending. They stress general values of honesty and truth instead of giving an evangelistic appeal, because religion was not allowed in public schools. The films did give students a theistic world view of the universe, and their sale helped to pay for other work of MIS which was definitely evangelistic.

To people in the Chicago radius, MBI means WMBI. Finances were a constant worry for the radio department as for the other areas of the Institute. Though business gradually picked up after the war, the tension in the world kept people in constant uncertainty, and the Institute income reflected the uncertainty. Finally, the radio began letting people know of financial needs, and many were surprised, thinking that since WMBI had not mentioned needs there were none!

The WDLM-FM station was discontinued in 1952 because of the relatively small listening audience. A few years later a group of Christian businessmen in Cleveland, Ohio, asked the Institute to operate a station in their area. The constant struggle for income made any expansion seem foolish. After deliberate prayer, the Institute agreed, but asked that the station be financed locally. The idea was that those who gave money would listen and continue to support the station. The FCC approved the license application, and Moody began broadcasting over WCRF in November 1958.

As finances improved, the radio department branched out still further. The next step was application for a permit to build an AM station in East Moline, Illinois. The call letters WDLM were used again and approved by the FCC, and the third Moody station went on the air in 1960.

At this time FM broadcasting throughout the country was growing so quickly that FM frequencies were getting scarce. The Institute trustees, aware of the trend, received permission to erect a noncommercial, educational FM station. It also went into operation in 1960.

If radio personnel sometimes wondered if anyone out there was listening, the answer came back a loud *yes* when the station was off the air for a week in May 1960. Though an announcement warned listeners repeatedly that work would be done on the AM tower, anxious callers flooded the switchboard with questions about the silence over WMBI. A couple even wondered if the rapture had taken place, and they had been left behind.

Through all the years the radio personnel struggled constantly to maintain FCC regulations and be professional in program quality and presentation. Moving from live to taped programs took tremendous pressure off performers. It also made for calmer nerves for control men who remember suddenly being aware of "dead air" when a faculty member was supposedly giving a Bible study. They rushed into the studio to find he had finished before the scheduled time and had gone back to his office. His explanation? "When the Holy Spirit stops, I stop."

Moving from the beginning years of only music and Bible programs, the radio ministry meets cultural, educational, information, and entertainment listener needs through news broadcasts, Social Security information, safety features, book reviews, and classical music programs. These in no way detract from the historically primary goals of strengthening the school and reaching the lost.

Where were the school's graduates? Scattered in many places and in varying kinds of work. So scattered, in fact, that the Alumni Association was practically nonexistent. Alumni simply were not enthusiastic about their school.

There were many reasons why alumni fellowships dropped from 34 in 1929 to 3 in 1948. The shortage of paper during the war cut the number of issues of the Alumni bulletin. War conditions made rallies and meetings impossible. Even the

1943 Alumni Founder's Week Luncheon was cancelled by rationing.

Then the first annual homecoming in May 1948 and the first issue of the new Alumni News set the association on the run. In a year the fellowships climbed from 3 to 32.

The annual giving increased as alumni interest continued to deepen. An alumni fund was set up to give a scholarship each year to two men and two women students at the end of their junior year.

Then in 1951 the alumni decided they wanted to recognize one outstanding alumnus each year, not for himself but for his service to the Lord. Dr. P. B. Fitzwater, a man who had poured his life back into the Institute, received the first annual Alumnus of the Year award.

But Dr. Culbertson's influence, like that of his predecessors, extended far beyond the physical campus, though it all related to the furthering of MBI. Even his connection with the Accrediting Association of Bible Colleges fit into his goals for his school.

The association came from the meeting of a group of Bible institute and Bible college officials who wanted to upgrade their academic standards and methods. Dr. Culbertson was a leading member of the planning group even though the Institute was not approved for membership until it moved to the semester plan in 1951.

Another side of his ministry was the radio messages given each week over WMBI. The half-hour taped messages went out later over stations in other cities. Dr. Culbertson's warm personality and the intensity of the message came through clearly. He taught deep scriptural truths, but his manner was so personal and conversational that his teaching came across as, "it's just the two of us talking together about the things of the Lord."

This tone was true also of the "Man to Man" records he made for busy pastors and Christian workers. The very practical nature of these messages from one pastor's heart to another comes through in this excerpt:

> Be very careful that truth is digested. Don't jump too quickly to preach on a text or a theme. Let it soak in; let it begin to live. Be willing to say, "It is not ready yet." Normally, to be ready to speak on anything at the drop of a hat is . . . shallowness, not profundity. . . . In all your getting of knowledge, make sure that whatever God is saying touches you and reaches you where you live.[13]

In addition to the many administrative responsibilities, the weekly chapel messages, and the radio and recording opportunities, his summers were busy with Bible conferences in this country and in Great Britain.

Dr. Culbertson also had a deep, quiet passion for missions. In 1952, he and Dr. Moon made a seven-week tour of the Near and Middle East, primarily photographing material for future films. At the request of several mission boards, he went to Africa and to the Far East. He had a great love for God's people, the Jews, and served on the advisory board of the American Association for Jewish Evangelism. This organization sponsored his several trips to the Holy Land.

Always on his travels, Dr. Culbertson looked for alumni, and always he found them, for the sun never sets on this part of Moody Bible Institute. He found Moody missionaries in the jungles of the inner city close by and in the remote man-forsaken jungles.

Dr. Culbertson anticipated the future as the calendar turned over to 1970. Proposals for branch evening schools, a new venture in the day school program, and participation in the 1972 Olympic Games project in Germany waited final developments. Though he led in the plans, others were to carry them out.

After years of guiding the school in a steady, stable growth, time came for his retirement. The board of trustees faced the job of selecting a new man. Dr. Culbertson remained as president until July 1971 and then moved to the newly created position of chancellor.

Eight years earlier he had had successful surgery for a malignancy, and had completely recovered. Then in May 1970, a spot on one lung put him in the hospital for surgery at the time *Pomp and Circumstance* brought faculty and graduates down the aisle in Torrey-Gray Auditorium. Again he recovered completely. Now, in 1971, he tired easily and had a nagging back pain which he tried to think was simply arthritis.

He conducted the inauguration of the new president, Dr. George Sweeting, the senior pastor of Moody Memorial Church, in September, but a few days later checked into Swedish Covenant Hospital. Tests showed the cancer had returned. From there God took him on November 16, just two days before his sixty-sixth birthday.

Dr. Sweeting's tribute at the funeral service was not simply to a man, but to a man of God.

> Dr. Culbertson was a steadfast and courageous soul. Though gracious and gentle, he was rock-like in his convictions. He surely was not a reed blown about by every new breeze. He loved the Word of God and passionately and wholeheartedly embraced the fundamentals of the faith.[14]

The students earlier that year had arranged a surprise "Culbertson Day" to express their love for him. Responding to their words to him, he said, "My prayer for you and for myself is that we end well."

For Dr. Culbertson the prayer was fully answered.

THE YOUNG STUDENT from the quiet, east coast town watched the traffic pouring along the streets. He pushed his way through the shoppers filling the Loop, and handed out tracts to the men shuffling along the sidewalk outside the mission doors. His heartbeat quickened at the excitement of city life.

But it was not only the bustle and opportunity of the city's activity that stirred his emotions. It was its need. Here was where the drums beat for him; not in the rural pastorate or the isolated mission field. This was the city as Mr. Moody had seen it with its culture and wealth, and its ignorance and poverty—people of all economic brackets in need of salvation.

George Sweeting's years as a student at Moody made certain God's call to the wasteland of American cities—if not Chicago, then another of America's neon-lit cities where men groped in darkness.

6

George Sweeting: Furthering
a Vision

THE WILD TUMULT and shouting in politics, on campuses, and in the streets faded to a sullen discontent that simmered under a surface quiet in the early 1970s.

The Vietnam War controversy lost some of its bitterness because of government assurances that the war was winding down. Troops did gradually withdraw, and then came out completely with the Vietnam peace agreement of 1973. This did not end the fear and misery for the Vietnamese, but it took away one of the issues so bitterly dividing Americans.

This war and the politics of the early seventies consumed the nation's energy. Newspaper stories made Mai Lai a familiar place. The killings at Kent State University and Jackson State College kept emotions running high.

Through it all, political campaign slogans promised to bring law and order, to erase crime in the streets, to clean out corruption in high places. But the promises proved empty hypocrisy when scandal toppled key officials, from the president on down. The Watergate corruption swept a broad net full of high officials who were responsible for breaking the laws they had sworn on the Bible to uphold. People became cynical about politics and contemptuous of politicians.

The government of the country transferred to Gerald Ford without obvious internal struggle or anxiety abroad. However, his pardon of Richard Nixon brought a storm of protest and raised questions about the whole amnesty issue. Worse still, the ordinary citizen discovered that the FBI and the CIA, agencies that he had long thought were keeping him safe, had been busy with secret surveillance of United States citizens.

Before the Watergate scandal broke open entirely, the president had made record-shattering trips abroad, opening the way for detente with Russia and for establishing diplomatic relations with Communist China. The United States moved from long-established Cold War relations with totalitarian countries to uneasy coexistence.

Other countries were still at one another's throats. A horrified world watched the television replay of the fatal invasion of the Israeli quarters at the 1972 Olympics in Munich. The senseless Yom Kippur War in Israel in October 1973 increased the danger of war in the Middle East. The following years escalated Arab-Israeli conflict with serious repercussions on the entire world.

Many other events made headlines to cause rejoicing or to raise fears. An assassination attempt paralyzed George Wallace while he campaigned before the 1972 presidential election. The United States had another moon landing, but this one brought either yawns from an apathetic public or cries of indigation that earth's problems needed the money and attention that was wasted on outer space. The energy crisis closed gasoline stations, raised gasoline prices, and lowered the speed limit on highways to save fuel. An unexpected bonus was the saving of lives that resulted because of fewer accidents.

The plight of frantic Vietnamese to get out of their devastated country touched Americans who opened hearts and homes. Relief poured in also for victims of the earthquake in Guatemala in 1976.

Social issues were no easier to solve in these years than they had been in previous eras. Plane hijackings and bombings and revolutionary ideas and methods dominated the news more than advances in social change or justice in the courts.

Children in public schools learned another kind of lesson as they sat home and watched striking teachers carry picket signs and chant slogans. Reaction to school busing laws in Boston showed the hatred underlying a polite surface tolerance. The Equal Rights Amendment, the abortion issue, the malpractice crisis, and the "right to die" question were hotly debated, only to remain unsolved. In 1975 the so-called Human Kindness Day in Washington, D.C., made headlines with muggings and thefts. Families planning bicentennial vacation trips to historical spots began to have second thoughts. Comic strips in newspapers satirized social and political issues.

These were still days of rage for some, but gradually the "under 30" mood shifted from protest to apathy or pragmatism. Young people needing employment faced a tight labor market. Suddenly college prep and business courses regained lost status. Styles in dress and general appearance continued to be casual, but some of the sloppiness of the previous decade lost its appeal. Job applicants trimmed hair, buttoned up their shirts, or wore dresses to make a good impression.

But the basic changes in attitude that came in the 1960s remained. The truth of Alexander Pope's lines,

> Vice is a monster of so frightful mien,
> As to be hated needs but to be seen;
> Yet seen too oft, familiar with her face,
> We first endure, then pity, then embrace,

shows in the permissiveness of the Age of Aquarius. An "anything goes" philosophy flooded every area of society. Trial marriages, communal living, deviate lifestyles, and excessive emphasis on sex had open approval.

The occult invaded the country, and Satan worshipers blatantly advertised their "church" services. Magazines, newspapers, movies, and television programs fed the obsession with readers and seers who claimed to foretell the future. Hare Krishna, Moon's Unification Church, and Children of God groups pestered passersby on street corners and in airports. Transcendental meditation captured imaginations and was even put into some public schools with its claim to be a science, not a religion.

All of this grew out of the revolt against authority, particularly against the authority of God's Word with its "Thou shalt not."

Oddly enough, this interest in a variety of religious experience brought a tolerance for Christianity and a willingness to listen to its claims. And people responded in different ways to different approaches.

The Bill Gothard Basic Youth Conflicts seminars drew thousands of participants of all ages from all levels of society. The appeal to young people of his "chain of command" principle astounded observers in view of the many flower children and communal families in the country.

Campus Crusade brought thousands thronging to Dallas, Texas, for Explo 72. Inter-Varsity's Urbana Conference in December 1973 again gathered a wide variety of evangelicals, with an emphasis still on world missions.

The charismatic movement swept across denominational lines, causing unrest and dissension in many quarters.

Politicians had always found it good business to speak favorably of God and sponsor prayer breakfasts. But a new depth of sincerity seemed to ring in the voices of some of the nation's leaders.

Growing dissatisfaction with public school methods and policies in discipline, reading material, and sex education caused many churches to begin private schools. Evangelical colleges and seminaries which kept a strong biblical stand turned away applicants, while liberal schools wondered aloud why they no longer attracted students.

Rereading Chicago newspaper headlines from 1970 on gives the impression that Watergate was the only important event in the country in those years. But other things were happening in the city also.

In 1969 State Street became a century old as an important shopping center, for the city's first department store had opened on the corner of State and Washington in 1869. While real estate in the shopping area remains high, suburban centers are eating into the Loop customer trade.

A massive face-lifting injected a sad note with the demolition of the Chicago Exchange Building, an 1893 landmark. Not so sad a note was the closing of the once bawling stockyards.

The 110-story Sears Tower soon outdistanced the 100-story John Hancock Building. These and the 83-story Standard Oil Building, plus other giants, brought Chicago a long way from its original cluster of small cabins.

Even though the city's facade looks impressive, it still urgently needs Mr. Crowell's Committee of Five to combat the growing menace of crime and vice. In some areas the pedestrian is bombarded with stores selling pornographic material or advertising nude shows. The Institute felt the impact of the vice when a bomb intended for a nearby massage parlor blew out windows in an Institute building.

Chicago politics made unexpected headlines when some long-entrenched city aldermen were convicted of various crimes and jailed. A grand jury went to work investigating the Black Panther police raid. And Mayor Daley won a sweeping sixth term victory.

Immigrants still respond to the appeal of Chicago. One man, a doctor in Poland, said, "What good is money and status if you have no freedom? I would rather work here as a janitor and be free. Chicago is the second homeland of the Polish people." One of the charms of Chicago is the ethnic neighborhoods which retain the distinctiveness of national heritage.

The city has come a long way socially, culturally, and economically since Mr. Moody put his school down in its center and sent his students out to evangelize it. But spiritually, its need is as great as it was then.

Moody Bible Institute had burst into life from Mr. Moody's desire to "fill Chicago with Christian workers." He worked unceasingly to do this through the school, Gospel literature, Bible classes, and conferences. So much went on in those busy, hectic years and so many opportunities waited that there was no time to stop and let planning catch up with vision.

But planning was essential, or the work would be all stem and no roots. So Dr. Torrey first, and then Dr. Gray dug deep to establish the curriculum and the learning-by-doing genius of Mr. Moody's enthusiasm. The Institute had to be well-grounded to stand against the strong winds of criticism.

Then the time was right again to stretch the Institute out across the world, not only through its students, but through films, radio, literature, and aviation. During the gloom of depression and anxiety of war, Dr. Houghton had carried Moody on with evangelistic energy.

Once more the times demanded a different pace, and Dr. Culbertson came to stabilize. He answered the clamor of riot and protest and rebellion against authority, constantly reminding the world that the unchanging Word remained valid in a world in ferment. In the stabilizing process, he gave a fresh look to curriculum and methods.

Now the future again waited with its challenge. Dr. Culbertson and the trustees wanted a man who would move into that challenge without deserting the heritage which had made the Moody Bible Institute unique. They wanted a pastor, an administrator, an evangelist, and yet a man who was committed to education.

God had ready, just a few blocks up the street, the senior pastor of Moody Memorial Church.

George Sweeting was born in 1924 in New Jersey. His parents prayed with and for their children and believed in disciplining in love. He accepted Christ as his Saviour as a young person and came as a student to the Institute. He graduated in 1945, the men's speaker for his class. He atended Gordon College in Massachusetts, and graduated in 1948, the president of his class. Later, Azuza Pacific College, Gordon-Conwell Divinity School, and Tennessee Temple College awarded him honorary doctoral degrees.

He married Hilda Schnell, also a Moody graduate, in 1947. A lovely, devoted helper, Mrs. Sweeting serenely provides a haven for him from his strenuous responsibilities. They and their four sons are a close-knit, loving family.

Dr. Sweeting became senior pastor of Moody Church after using his Moody training as a pastor and evangelist across the country. A little news item in an earlier *Moody Alumni News* said simply, "George Sweeting, '45 has entered evangelistic work seven months ago and has experienced the blessing of the Lord on his ministry." He needed every bit of past experience in his ministry at Moody Church, which had been without a pastor for over three years. Under Dr. Sweeting the church revived. While pastor there, he served as the Institute alumni representative on the board of trustees.

With his retirement just around the corner, Dr. Culbertson personally spoke to him about becoming president and the trustees made the request official in January 1971. Dr. Sweeting accepted with the words, "My confidence is in Christ alone who is all-sufficient."

Even before his formal installation on September 28, 1971, he plunged into plans for growth. The words in Acts 2:17 became his as he challenged fellow employees to dream dreams and see visions of what God waited to do through the Institute in the years ahead.

Other members of administration caught his enthusiasm and set goals for the next fifteen years, leading to the Institute's centennial in 1986. These plans were compiled, and Dr. Sweeting presented them formally to the board of trustees.

From his experience as a pastor came his conviction that the challenge confronting the church for the seventies was "to intelligently present Jesus Christ to the secular world." For this challenge the Institute had unlimited resources, as he reminded his fellow employees in his 1971 inaugural address, "Visions and Dreams."

> It is our intention to pray and strive for a high intelligent spirit of evangelism to permeate every area of the Moody Bible Institute. It is our prayer that God will use this ministry to stimulate world revival and world evangelism during the last part of this twentieth century. This is to be accomplished through our faculty, administration, employees and students. We will utilize the *Moody Monthly* magazine, Moody Press, Moody Literature Mission, Moody radio, Moody aviation, and Moody Institute of Science.

A first priority in putting the plan to work was to secure a broader base of support, a recurring theme ever since Mr. Moody's day. Mr. Moody faced the need for money as did Dr. Gray—and then Dr. Houghton—and Dr. Culbertson. The Institute required more money to operate than most schools, because of the tuition-free training it provides every student. Even a very conservative figure of $2,000 a year for each student multiplied by 1,300 students makes a staggering $2,600,000 each year that must be prayed in for education alone. This is the burden which Institute leaders constantly carry.

Moody's name encircles the globe through its students. But many people have only a fuzzy idea of what the Institute could mean to them through radio, films, and literature. So Dr. Sweeting proposed a nation-wide radio broadcast to acquaint people with the Institute and, through it, with Jesus Christ.

> It is our purpose to present the message and the ministry of

the Moody Bible Institute. This broadcast would convey the gospel message. We intend it to be a straightforward, relevant, hard hitting, intelligent approach. . . . The purpose of this broadcast would be to proclaim the gospel, to enlist new students and recruit interested donors, to extend the outreach of *Moody Monthly* as well as all the ministries of the Moody Bible Institute. This broadcast could become an important link to all our ministries.

These plans took shape and became *Moody Presents,* a weekly half-hour program which features a message by Dr. Sweeting, good music, a report on some part of the Institute, and a student testimony.

Global outreach plans came next. The first was student participation in a project for the 1972 Olympics in Munich. Here history repeated itself. When Mr. Moody heard of Chicago's World's Fair plans, he exclaimed that it was an opportunity of a lifetime for a Christian witness. The Munich Olympic Project was another opportunity to use a man-made event to present the world with the claims of Christ. This time the interest catcher was MIS films.

Fifty Moody students were specially trained to counsel those attending the film showings. Even the tragic killing of Israeli participants opened unexpected opportunities, for it sobered many and made them willing to listen to the gospel.

A similar project at Montreal in the summer of 1976 followed the same successful Munich idea.

A visit was made to Great Britain in December 1973 to January 1974, by invitation of British Christian leaders. The purpose? To retrace Mr. Moody's steps through his great evangelistic crusade in 1873 and 1874, when "a spirit of evangelism was awakened that has never died away." Dr. Sweeting, the Moody Chorale, and a team of students from the evangelism major spoke and sang in churches, in civic centers, at school assemblies, and on street corners in the cities that so long ago had felt the touch of God through Moody and Sankey. The Dutch Television Network, at its own expense, taped the team's two-hour London rally.

Dr. Sweeting shared Mr. Moody's burden for city evangelism. In fact, this concern brought the Moody Bible Institute into being in 1886. Moody had said, "Either these people are to be evangelized, or the leaven of communism and infidelity will assume such enormous proportions that it will break out in a reign of terror such as this country has never known." The events of the following years showed how prophetic Moody's words were. As the city grew, the leaven of sin grew also in those "enormous proportions."

So in 1974, students, staff, and cooperating churches joined to help fulfill the dream that was part of the very bricks of the buildings—reaching Chicago for Christ.

A personal letter from Dr. Sweeting went first to 400,000 homes on the north side of Chicago. The letter outlined the plan of salvation in simple, clear words and offered a free, specially prepared correspondence lesson entitled, "The Good Life." The thousands who answered the letter later opened their front doors to a personal witness. Visitation teams of staff and students joined teams from thirty churches, and went out to homes two by two. A huge rally at Medinah Temple wrapped up the 1974 Chicago Evangelism Outreach. Similar plans reached the west side of the city in 1975 and plans have been made to reach the south side.

But none of the outreach emphases took the place of the heart of the work, the school. One constant feature, sometimes overlooked in the more spectacular accomplishments of radio and literature and films, are the classes which meet regularly each day. While newspaper headlines splash news of floods, moon landings, medical advances, and political change, students daily discover "God's News behind the news" in the Word of God.

Of course there is more to a school than classes. Students learn from each other in casual conversations in the cafeteria line, in heated late-night discussions in the dorms, from PCW (Practical Christian Work) assignments, and from employment responsibilities. But the undergirding should take place in the classroom from men and women who have gone through the furnace of disciplined study and know beyond a shadow of a doubt "whom they have believed."

Some schools base faculty evaluation on a "publish or perish" notion, or on the number of study trips abroad a teacher makes. Moody teachers are judged first of all on their personal commitment to Jesus Christ. No consideration is given anyone who has not accepted Jesus Christ as his personal Saviour. Beyond this must be complete agreement with the doctrinal position of the Institute.

In the years since Moody's founding, unbelief tore many holes in the cloth of the nation's fath, all aimed at destroying the Bible. Many institutions turned from faith in the infallibility of Scripture and forever lost opportunities for greatness. The personal history of the Moody Bible Institute shows that God honors those who honor His Word.

In the crisis years before the first World War and then during the unrest in the 1920s, a doctrinal statement was written to make the Institute's stand clear to all. It includes belief in the Bible as the Word and Revelation of God; in the Deity of the Lord Jesus Christ, His virgin birth, His death as a substitute, His physical resurrection and bodily ascension, and His coming again; in the Personality and Deity of the Holy Spirit; and in the mission of the church to evangelize the world.

A standard of holiness is difficult to set in these days of wide varieties of lifestyles and shifting standards. But faculty are expected to obey the command of Titus 2:12 to "live soberly, righteously, and godly, in this present world" because of their expectation of "the glorious appearing of the great God and our Saviour Jesus Christ."

Faculty members are chosen for their scholarship, with an emphasis on those who have earned degrees. God is not content with mediocrity, and those who serve Him should not be either. Totally yielded scholarship and genuine spirituality go hand in hand.

A climate of freedom in the classroom requires the principle God used as He kept the distinctive abilities of those through whom He gave His Word. Teachers are not hired laborers; they are specialists committed to the challenge of helping young people "be no more children, tossed to and fro, and carried about with every wind of doctrine, . . . But speaking the truth in love, may grow up into him in all things, which is the head, even Christ" (Ephesians 4:14-15).

The goal is that administration, faculty, and students be bonded by open communication. They are together in the battle against Satan, who so often masquerades as an angel of light.

Teaching methods change, equipment improves, classes become smaller. The old lecture room of days gone by is only a memory. Much valuable learning took place in those large classes through Chicago's bitterly cold winters and sticky, hot summers. Often the teachers were revered men, respected, sometimes feared, but not always thought of as friends.

The personal contacts of teachers and students in smaller classes is beyond value. To keep this personal touch alive, administration looks for men and women with earned doctorates representing scholarship, who are committed to teaching the Word, and who can be an example to others. No standard is too high in view of the responsibility Moody faculty have to be examples to the students who come.

And students mark their years at school by those who taught them. Alumni coming back to visit look for the teachers who made the school. As alumni they wanted to show their appreciation of the faculty, so the Alumni Association inaugurated a Faculty Citation which recognizes one teacher each year for his classroom teaching and his out-of-class contacts. Only one faculty member each year receives the award, but each one represents others who could have been selected for the honor.

The faculty welcomed 1,300 students to rejuvenated dormitories in the fall of 1974. The complete renovation of old, familiar Osborne Hall gave colorful rooms to women students. And another old building previously had been made new. For months employees had watched the changes in the interior of Smith Hall, which dated back before World War I. Floors, walls, and stairways disappeared, leaving only a shell of a building. This was carefully rebuilt to give modern facilities for the Health Service, dormitory rooms for women and married couples, *Moody Monthly* offices, and much needed faculty offices. Graduates returning for Founder's Week looked in vain for the stairs they once climbed and the elevators they waited for and exclaimed over the vivid reception room that once had been old-fashioned, dark Massey Chapel.

Some of the new students in the 1970s were part of a new program. Before Dr. Culbertson's retirement, the education department had dreamed of beginning a specialized program for college graduates that would be separate from the rest of the courses. A phenomenon of the times is the great number of college students on secular campuses who come to know Christ as Saviour and want to serve Him on mission fields. Many of them come from nominally Christian or even pagan American homes, knowing nothing about the Bible; so mission boards recommend that they get at least a year of Bible training. Moody began its Advanced Studies Program for just such college graduates, offering thirty hours of post-baccalaureate work in an intensive one-year study.

Some of the graduates of this specialized program are already active on mission fields adding their lives to the many others who trained at the Moody Bible Institute.

Regardless of the program or major students enroll in, the standards for admission remain the same. Mr. Moody had called for "consecrated men and women who were willing to give all to God." This is still the call. The emphasis on Christian character that appeared in the 1895 catalog appears in the 1976 and will in the next and the next until the Lord comes and there is no longer a need for such a demand because "we shall be like Him."

The saying, "The more things change, the more they remain the same," is true, for Moody's original goal of giving training in Bible, music, and practical Christian work remains the same. Still—not exactly the same. Though students go out as always on assignments, the PCW office tries to be selective and gear experience to the student's ability and his major.

Practical Christian work traditionally has meant visiting in hospitals and jails, teaching Bible classes, working with children, taking part in mission meetings, passing out tracts. But it also includes the Good Samaritan projects of raking leaves, putting up storm windows, or reading to the elderly. This is not new, for Mr. Moody took baskets of food and buckets of coal along with his hearty, "Come to church" invitations.

The missionary emphasis at Moody, though one of its strongest commitments, is not just for the student when he finishes school and flies off to another culture in a far country. It is a here and now opportunity on a PCW assignment. Each week approximately 2,400 day and evening school students go into the mission field of Chicago and its suburbs to every possible ethnic, social, political, economic, and religious culture.

The second feature, music, still rings through the total school life. It touches all students either through classwork, group singing in meetings, or concerts by the school musical groups.

These groups are an integral part of the Institute. The Auditorium Choir, organized at Dr. Gray's request, was later renamed the Moody Chorale and began to build the reputation for excellence it has today. The Women's Glee Club and Handbell Choir, the Men's Glee Club, and the Concert Band carry on the same tradition of excellence.

The third emphasis, the study of the Bible, remains the most important. No matter what his chosen major is, whether it is music or missionary aviation or pastoral training, each student has concentrated Bible study. The rather hackneyed comment is true that *Bible* is the Institute's middle name.

Administration and faculty come back repeatedly to reinforce the statement in the 1922-23 catalog that no matter how gifted a student may be in speaking, in music, and even in soul winning, "if he be not grounded in the Word of God he cannot be an entirely safe leader among men, nor can he truly glorify God in his service."

Belief in the inerrancy of God's Word is as crucial an issue today as it was when Dr. Torrey faced it, and Dr. Gray, and Dr. Houghton, and Dr. Culbertson. Then it was the liberal theologian and the higher critic who broke from a literal interpretation. Today more and more evangelicals believe that the Bible is only partially trustworthy. This could affect the very foundation of Christianity. Moody Bible Institute is firmly committed to the absolute dependability of the Bible as the very Word of God and stands on this in the training of its students and in the ministry of its every department.

The Evening School continued to widen its circle as interest in adult education made branch schools essential. The first of these was an evening extension school in Joliet, Illinois, staffed by Institute faculty. The next year a school began in Elgin, Illinois, its classes also taught by Institute teachers. A third school opened in Akron, Ohio. Because of its distance from Chicago, this evening branch has a full-time resident coordinator and uses local pastors as teachers with a minimum of help from Institute personnel.

Enrollment multiplied in the evening sessions on the main Chicago campus. In spite of the talk of "fear cities"—a reputation deserved by Chicago and other large cities—students still come at night to study. The Institute provides well-lighted, off-the-street, guarded parking to help evening school students walk safely.

Why do they come? The students themselves answer: "I didn't know how to live the Christian life, because I didn't know God's Word until I came to evening classes." Another said, "I had lost my wife and was trying to raise my children and work. Things were getting out of control. But at the end of the day, after I had checked on my children, I knew that if I could get down to Moody, everything would be all right."

The adult education interest is also reflected in the growth of the Correspondence School. Its courses range from the very elementary to those on the college level. Some colleges give transfer credit for the college-level courses. Some of the correspondence courses are on a graduate level and take from two to three years to complete.

When Dr. Torrey planned the correspondence courses, he made them convenient for people to study while riding the streetcar to and from work. Today's correspondence students have audio cassette tapes for their convenience. Now those who have always wanted to take a New Testament Greek course and cannot enroll in school can get a correspondence school tape and study by mail.

Many thousands in the Chicago area and in other cities know of the Correspondence School and the Day and Evening schools because of the radio network.

Radio has come a long way from the days when people sat with headsets clamped over their ears, straining to hear the scratchy sounds coming over the airwaves—such a marvel! Now WMBI broadcasts in stereo, and listeners take the smooth, silken tones for granted.

But the quality of the sound, while important, is not the main goal; reaching listener needs is. And letters pour in telling how needs were met. One lady, after hearing a Bible study, wrote: "God knew I needed those words just at that precise time. Isn't it wonderful that He had you say them the very day I needed them." But that Bible study had been given two years earlier, taped, and rerun. The living power of God's Word is a daily miracle.

Moody was a pioneer in gospel broadcasting, breaking ground for Christian communicators around the world. HCJB in Quito, Ecuador, and Trans World Radio in Bonaire, Netherlands Antilles, use Moody-produced programs regularly in their worldwide shortwave broadcasts.

In July 1973, Chicago's WLS-TV aired a five-minute prime-time news special featuring WMBI which, according to WLS was "on the air when radio was a novelty." One reporter coming to write a story could not understand how Aunt Theresa's "KYB (Know Your Bible) Club," the longest running Chicago radio program, had kept such interest with its simple and dull—to him—format.

Three other stations came into the radio network. First WMBW in Chattanooga, Tennessee, which broadcasts into five states. Then in 1974, KMBI AM-FM opened in Spokane, Washington. Back in 1958 the broadcasting department found that moving into a new community and making friends was not any easier for radio stations than for people. So friends of the Institute formed a Cleveland Radio Fellowship to build a smooth working relationship between the station and the community. Chattanooga and Spokane formed similar committees.

When WMBI began, foreign broadcasts were an important feature and then were discontinued. But interest in this kind of outreach revived. After all, the missions emphasis in the school included the Cabrini-Green housing project as well as Africa or South America. The same principle should hold true for the radio. It could not talk of needs across the world in Spain and ignore the 700,000 Spanish-speaking people within the WMBI listening area. So the schedule included a block of Spanish language programming.

Radio personnel facing mute microphones or pulling

switches sometimes wonder, Is anybody out there really listening? Complaints come when someone goofs or when a listener disagrees with a program. But who else listens? Letter week is one way of finding out. The first such week in 1929 brought 5,375 letters. Letter week 1976 poured 55,000 letters across the desks of grateful radio staff members. The response came not just from Chicago fans, but from listeners in small towns and big cities where radio stations count on Moody to fill their time slots with quality programs.

Though the letters came in response to the broadcasting department's letter week appeal, they gave a lift to other departments as well. *Inflation* and *recession* were more than mere words to businessmen; publishers among them. In spite of high costs and paper shortages, Moody Press went on about its business of continuing to carry out one of Mr. Moody's most enthusiastic dreams. In 1973 it shipped more than enough books to overflow a fifty-car train with 40,000 pounds of books per car.

Moody Press reached a new level of recognition among Christian booksellers when *Daktar/Diplomat in Bangladesh, Satan in the Sanctuary,* and *Love, Honor, and Be Free* made the Christian best seller lists. The Press became a distributor of the New American Standard Bible. The most ambitious project in Moody Press history has been the *Wycliffe Bible Encyclopedia,* which was released in 1975 after years of careful writing and editing.

To say that nearly ten million Moody Press publications were purchased and read in 1975 is a cold fact until it comes to life in a man who learned to pray through reading a Moody Press book, a child who found the importance of being friendly, a woman who found Christ as her Saviour. These experiences were common to people in Germany, Sweden, Finland, Holland, Korea, and Japan who read Moody Press books in their own languages. Each book has the power to change lives in some way, helping people of all ages and life-styles make a total commitment to Christ.

When the idea of Moody Literature Mission began in 1894, the world was vastly different. It took months for books to reach their destination. Then they were not widely read, for the literacy rate was low. But in this jet-propelled, computerized world where the mass media bombards the senses with sight and sound stimuli, a religious book faces an uphill battle to catch the interest of a blasé public. Moody Literature Mission boldly meets the challenge of reshaping the minds of men.

In an effort to influence America's political leaders in these crucial years, MLM gave a copy of Viggo Olsen's *Daktar/Diplomat in Bangladesh* to the president, his cabinet members, and every member of Congress. They also received Dr. Sweeting's book, *Love Is the Greatest*; and the new book by Robert Flood, director of *Moody Monthly, America, God Shed His Grace on Thee,* because of its appeal during the bicentennial year.

Moody Literature Mission has never been a respecter of persons. It reaches political leaders, and those who are slaves to drugs or liquor; rich parents in American suburbs, and orphaned children begging on streets in India.

When a gift of money comes in earmarked for MLM—five dollars—fifteen—sixty—it suddenly multiplies and takes different shapes. It may become an Arabic tract, or a hymnal in a tribal language, or perhaps a Christian storybook for Korean children. Some of the money may provide Spanish literature for prisons in El Salvador.

One of the pet projects of MLM is providing free Christian fiction for classroom libraries in public schools. One teacher wrote of how "greedy" she was for these books for her children. Another told how ragged from use the Moody books looked on the bookshelves. MLM sends Gospels of John as teachers request them for rewards for their children.

Mr. Moody's special burden was to put literature behind prison walls, and that continues. But another project just getting under way puts literature in another kind of prison, the nursing homes. Large-print books for easy reading help fill the lonely hours that stretch between relatives' visits.

Another Institute publication firmly established itself as one of the nation's top Christian magazines. *Moody Monthly* more than doubled its circulation in four years, reaching 250,000 subscribers. The climbing subscription figures are important not for numbers alone, but as evidence that the Christian magazine can influence the secular world.

In an era when many religious publications are folding, the *Chicago Tribune* cited *Moody Monthly* as an exception. The magazine was named "Periodical of the Year" in 1976 by the Evangelical Press Association.

Moody Monthly's dress and shape are now quite different from what they were when Dr. Torrey and Dr. Gray became coeditors back in 1907. Then the few pictures were black and white and not too clear, the print was small, the pages were crowded. Now its new design and graphics catch even the casual eye.

But a magazine must offer more than a colorful appearance to have any lasting impact, and *Moody Monthly* does. The editors have retained the goals set many years ago of informing readers of what is happening in the Christian world, reinforcing the ministry of the local church, promoting sound doctrine, strengthening the Christian family, giving Bible study, serving as a voice of leadership and conviction in the Christian world. And God has honored the magazine.

Newsstands on street corners and in drugstores have generally featured women's magazines, sports magazines, general interest magazines, fiction, and—regretfully—an increasing amount of pornography. Now this age of tolerance extends even to a willingness to have evangelical literature on magazine racks. This opens a new market to make *Moody*

Monthly's clear witness for Christ available to a so far untouched segment of the population.

Another part of America's population being touched by the Institute is the thousands of school children who see MIS films. A recent film, *Where the Waters Run,* shows how important water is to life and makes the clear application to Christ, the Water of life. MIS produced a series of six color and sound educational filmstrips based on *Water.* Each filmstrip was carefully coordinated with the science curriculum for use in public schools. The series emphasizes that God is the Creator of the water we take for granted but which is essential to life. A spurt in the sale of these educational films means that thousands of children are seeing films which show God as the Creator of the universe; perhaps the film is the only antidote to evolution that some children get.

MIS dreams of reaching adults in the same way on prime time United States network television. Contracts have already been made for a thirteen-week television series of Sermons from Science films. Foreign television stations have aired Moody films in Argentina, Australia, Ecuador, Haiti, Honduras, Mexico, Peru, and Japan. In fact, MIS was the first gospel programming aired on Tokyo TV, reaching an audience estimated at five million.

In the Beginning . . . God is the title of the newest MIS film. But, in a sense it is not new at all; at least the idea is not. This film ties together all that Moody Institute of Science—and Moody Bible Institute—has stood for since its very first film, *The God of Creation.* The emphasis on God's sovereignty in the world and in individual lives has been the breath of the Institute since its founding.

This insistent belief that God has a personal interest in His creation motivates the Extension Department as it follows the Acts 1:8 pattern. All the Moody Bible Institute witness begins at home in Chicago and then spreads out to the world.

Moody is very much a picture of the Christian who is to be

in the world but not *of* it. The Institute is in the city but not of it. It is an integral part of its surroundings which crowd close to its doors, and students go out to this "Jerusalem," of which they choose to become a part for three years.

The greatest outreach into Chicago comes from student efforts and from the radio broadcasts. In addition, faculty and staff members are in constant demand to fill pulpits. The majority of these preaching opportunities take place within one hundred miles of Chicago.

From here the witness spreads across the country in Institute-sponsored conferences, and in camps and individual preaching or musical meetings. Prophetic conferences draw thousands who come to find assurance of God's eternal purposes.

In November 1974, the "uttermost parts" were reached again as Dr. Sweeting led an evangelistic team to Mexico City; Guatemala City; Quito, Ecuador; Bogata, Columbia; and the Netherlands Antilles to meet national Christians, strengthen Moody missionary alumni, and see firsthand what God was doing in foreign missions.

But the travel pattern is also reversed as people come *to* Chicago for conferences. Founder's Week continues its impact with crowds overflowing Torrey-Gray Auditorium. This February conference is necessarily geared to a wide range of needs because of the varied interests of the people who attend. Pastors coming to the conference traditionally have had special afternoon sessions to answer their problems and give them encouragement. From this the idea came: Why not have a conference solely for pastors?

In 1973, Dr. Sweeting presented his dream for a pastors' conference to the trustees. He expected two or three hundred pastors to attend. Over six hundred came from 41 denominations and 37 states, and from Puerto Rico, Canada, and Scotland. The conference took place before the summer school began, and the pastors stayed in the dormitories, ate in the student dining room, and were fed intellectually and spiritually in day and evening sessions. The conference more than proved its value in the next two years, as the attendance shot up to a thousand, filling the dormitories to capacity. Numbers do not tell the entire story, of course, but they are the thermometer which registers the effectiveness of the program.

Back when Mr. Moody began his work, Chicago did not number in the millions, and newspapers were eager to tell of citizens' accomplishments. Mr. Moody was a world traveler; a man who made things happen. Privately, reporters may have laughed at his queer ideas, but they gave his work publicity.

Then the city population multiplied; its people became more sophisticated. Newspapers were less interested in reporting religious news, especially news of what some considered a "store-front" variety. And so Moody Bible Institute generally was bypassed by the media.

In recent years, observers began to have new respect for MBI as they saw property improvements. New, attractive buildings replaced old; ivy climbed women's dorm walls; shrubbery lined paved, lighted parking lots; flowers and trees bloomed in the interior campus; polite, neatly dressed young people went in and out the doors. In October 1973, Mayor Daley presented MBI a Chicago Beautiful Award in recognition of "significant contributions to beautification of the City."

Other awards have come spontaneously. Montgomery Ward presented its 1974 Humanitarian Award to Moody students for tutoring children in the Cabrini-Green Housing Project. And the YMCA Youth Service Award recognized the community service Institute students gave through the Big Brother-Big Sister Program, calling the Moody student body one of the "greatest assets of the near north side of Chicago."

Other contacts have been instigated by city officials. As Chicago prepared for the annual Christmas parade down State Street in 1973, someone suddenly realized at the last minute that the parade had no float which portrayed the real meaning of Christmas.

A frantic call to the Institute gave students and staff time to put together a beautiful float with the theme, "Wise Men Still Seek Him." The invitation was repeated in 1974—though not at the last minute—and the spirit of Christmas was captioned in the words, "No Room in the Inn." The school now has an annual invitation to have a float in the Christmas parade, with no restrictions on the theme.

Another opportunity came when city officials invited the combined musical groups to present a concert at the Civic Center Plaza during the noon hour when crowds filled the streets.

The secular media provided an unexpected voice for the Institute message in a variety of ways in the last few years. A WLS-TV news special which featured WMBI noted that it had been "following the basic Bible line right down through the years." WGN radio featured the dean of education on "Extension 720," a radio talk show, in January 1974 and again in 1975. Though paired in discussions with extremely liberal ministers, he had opportunity to present and defend the reasonableness of a literal interpretation of Scripture and to give the plan of salvation as listeners called in their comments. CBS-TV featured another member of faculty in a panel discussion on the occult. And WBBM aired a series of spot interviews on the purpose of Moody Bible Institute.

Channel 2 sent newsmen with camera crews to "try to find out how in a world of secularism, a place like MBI could exist, much less flourish." Ten hours of filming and interviewing people from the president to the maintenance staff was compressed into a six-minute story on the six o'clock evening news.

The *Sun-Times Midwest* magazine carried a cover story on the Institute with three full pages of copy and color pictures. A major story appeared on the front page of the *Chicago*

Tribune, and other Chicago papers have initiated articles on the Institute and its activities.

Publicity in the press is not a new thing for the Institute. Mr. Moody was news wherever he went, not because of himself, but because he was the bearer of good news. This kind of publicity is an open door of witness. And it lets people know that in a city where wickedness abounds, God's grace abounds even more in the buildings on Chicago and LaSalle.

The buildings filling the block on LaSalle Street, north from Chicago Avenue and west to Wells Street, have stood steady through the years, symbolic of the training that gave security to many students.

Years ago, the first student yearbook editor searched for a name that would really express what Moody Bible Institute stood for. She tried the sound of many but discarded them. Finally, wandering restlessly around the campus, hearing typewriters clacking, seeing teachers and students huddled in the shadows of the old buildings, she crossed the LaSalle Street traffic and looked back at the buildings leaning against the skyline.

And there it was, the feature that was MBI—the Arch. Through it had come and gone people who learned the truth of "except a corn of wheat fall into the ground and die, it abideth alone" (Jn 12:24) —young people like John and Betty Stam.

Others learned that serving God did not necessarily bring fame and glory—like the single missionary who lived with loneliness in the Kentucky hills or the couple enduring the bite of Alaska winters.

Still others became famous as evangelists, pastors, writers, and musicians who brought many to righteousness. But whether known or unknown, those who have passed through Moody's arch carry the truth of Daniel 11:32, "but the people that do know their God shall be strong, and do exploits."

For God, who commanded the light to shine out of darkness, hath shined in our hearts, to give the light of the knowledge of the glory of God in the face of Jesus Christ. But we have this treasure in earthen vessels, that the excellency of the power may be of God, and not of us (2 Corinthians 4:6-7).

THE SHRIEK OF POLICE SIRENS in the oppressive summer heat swallowed the clattering noise of the typewriter. The girl listened, a longing for her quiet southern town lapping at the edge of memory. Surely there were easier ways to serve God than in a stifling office typing endless reports. Then came the words of that morning's devotions: "Even Christ pleased not Himself." She began the staccato rhythm again, knowing she could not lightly discard her call to work at Moody Bible Institute. . . .

The electrician worked patiently but quickly to repair the short in the maze of wires frayed by age and use. The speaker in the crowded auditorium could not continue without his skill. The electrician smiled at the challenge. Private industry offered a larger salary, but not a greater satisfaction. . . .

The swish-slap of brushes as painters transformed dingy walls—the hum of machinery in the copy center, the print plant, the service department, the carpenter shop—books and tracts packed for far-off places—the careful preparation of lessons in Bible, Greek, missions, music. . . .

All this done by earthen vessels through whose lives God worked to show His power and glory.

7

Employees: Supporting a Vision

THE HISTORY of the Moody Bible Institute does not revolve only around its presidents, important as their leadership is. It is not seen alone in the financial wisdom of the board of trustees, or in the officers' ability to wisely direct its multiple ministries. Its true history lies embedded in the host of men and women—earthen vessels—who gave their lives to the work.

Out of the shadows of the past step these people. Some who came in answer to God's invitation served a few brief years; others remained a lifetime. Some are remembered because they often stood in the limelight, preaching in Torrey-Gray auditorium, directing musical groups, singing and playing instruments. Others sat for long hours at typewriters, pushed brooms, moved chairs, loaded dishwashers, handled laundry, packed books in a dusty warehouse; their names forgotten because they were not written in anyone's book except God's.

Sometimes their work seemed unappreciated, acknowledged only in a meager salary check. Those who came young and eager grew old and gray as the years went by. The words of Dr. Houghton's song proved true:

> The world moves on, so rapidly the living
> The forms of those who disappear replace,
> And each one dreams that he will be enduring—
> How soon that one becomes the missing face!

But the gratitude was always there, undergirding every sacrifice of time and effort and salary. An annual report just at the end of the second World War put the thanks into words for one department and were echoed in every other department.

> With few exceptions, the full-time employees . . . have done great work under great difficulties. This is also true of many of the student helpers. But I should like to pay special tribute to the full-time mechanics and janitors who have worked so faithfully, quietly, and hard behind the scenes. Though shorthanded, they have made major alterations, working all night at times to make repairs. Head janitors have worked long, hard hours, sometimes without crews. These men have turned their backs on highly remunerative employment obtainable elsewhere, to stand loyally by, because they love the Lord and the Institute. We owe them a large debt of gratitude.

God speaks in Hebrews 12 of the "great cloud of witnesses" who surround us. Some of these are listed in the Hebrews 11 Hall of Fame. But imagination pictures this cloud as including a great host of unnamed believers down through the ages.

Whole chapters in the Old Testament are simply lists of names. We skip over them with some impatience; they are unknown to us and so we consider them unimportant. Not God—no one is unimportant in His reckoning, and no one remains unnamed in His Book.

The files at MBI contain names—names which reveal faces and personalities. From 1886 to the present, a swelling tide of people served as secretaries, cooks, janitors, teachers, administrators, typists, editors, receptionists, and printers. They span the years that took the Institute from its first faltering steps to its present confident stride. They form a great crowd, another "cloud of witnesses," too many to be mentioned individually. But from their ranks step representative lives.

Some of them were faculty, important to the school. Sharing

in the early beginnings were William R. Newell and R. A. Torrey. The first Moody graduate, William Evans, came back to teach. H. H. McGranahan began to build the music faculty, followed immediately by D. B. Towner, composer of thousands of songs including "Trust and Obey" and "At Calvary." William Runyan gave "Great Is Thy Faithfulness," a hymn which has become inseparably linked with Institute memories of answered prayer.

As the work grew, other men of God, many of them Moody graduates, came to teach the Word clearly. They include the stern but beloved P. B. Fitzwater who gave his wealth of Bible knowledge for over forty years, H. Framer Smith, R. H. Glover, Alfred Holzworth, Max Reich, Guy Latchaw, T. J. Bittikofer, and George S. Schuler, whose "Make Me A Blessing" is still a blessing. Kenneth S. Wuest gave pastor's course men a love for Greek.

We remember William Hockman, John Riebe, Harold Cook, who was "Mr. Missions" to many students, Nathan Stone, Adella Dunlap, Elgin S. Moyer, Donald P. Hustad, Harold and Arvilla Garner who lived Christian Education, Helen Needham, G. Coleman Luck, Wilfred Burton, Arthur Springer, and Harry Dixon Loes, who is remembered for "All Things in Jesus." S. Maxwell Coder was dean of education during the crucial move into the degree program. Grace Darling and Gladys Mary Talbot each gave over thirty years of themselves to the "school that D. L. Moody founded."

The files of the dean of students' department bring from the long past the names of Sarah Capron, Charlotte Cary, and Annie Rosie; well-loved matrons. The small chapel in Culbertson Hall, the men's dormitory, is named in honor of A. Franklin Broman, dean of men for many years.

Ruby Jackson for 38 years guided students through the intricacies of registration. And James F. Harrison, Helen Rentschler, Alice E. Heck, and Alice E. Everard contributed a combined 130 years of enthusiastic work.

The Correspondence School grew under W. Taylor Joyce, William H. Lee Spratt, Philip Newell, and Herbert Klingbeil whom God took home long before his fellow employees thought his work was finished. There also quiet, faithful Eleanor Ostlund served for forty-one years, and Sammie Hogue edited manuscripts with her kind but decisive blue pencil.

Moody Press and the Colportage Department came alive under William Runyan, Norman Camp, and J. D. Hall. Elizabeth Thompson came to that department, an eager, just-turned-eighteen-year old, and stayed to receive a fifty-year service pin from Dr. Culbertson, her eyes and smile and wit still sparkling. There Kenneth Taylor and Peter Gunther combined a vision for literature outreach that surpassed even Mr. Moody's dreams.

In the carpenter shop Rudolph Rossler's skilled hands worked with tools for forty-nine years. Though not known by name to the visitors who passed him in the halls, God recognized his labor of love. As He did also that of Alice Anderson, a secretary for fifty-one years; Gertrude Germann's fifty-five years of service; Grace Boman's years in the *Moody Monthly* office; Gertrude Draves' gracious service in many capacities for thirty-five years; Margaret Hutchison in the dining room; Thomas Gilmer, a technician in radio; and Nettie Cox so conscientiously handling the Institute's printed materials. Arnold Krueger gave forty-two years to the Lord at Moody, including in his last years a stint as a parking lot attendant where his smile remained radiant even in the worst weather.

Homes all across the country anticipated the blessing of visits from stewardship men like Howard Nelson, Donald G. Hescott, Merkel Good, Harold Stephens, and Henry Kraakevik.

Radio personalities Wendell Loveless, "Uncle John" Meredith, Robert Parsons, Theresa Worman, and Frances Youngren, whose voices were familiar friends in many homes, would be the first to give credit to the receptionists, the sound men, the announcers, and the engineers who dovetailed what might have been incoherent sounds into a pattern of harmony.

Others who must be recognized are Carl Schumacher, William Lessel, Myrtle Craig, John Raymond, Leonard Unkefer, and E. C. Christiansen, whose wife Avis has given a rich heritage of hymns.

Space limitations permit only the mention of secretaries May Hogan, Martha Wetherbee, Ruth Egre, and Mildred Wilkie, who served with LeRoy Johnson, Earl Anderson, and H. E. Stockburger, whose wise handling of the budget made money stretch to impossible lengths.

Credit must go to C. B. Nordland, whose wisdom stepped him into a wide variety of positions. And it was largely the vision and plans and prayers of Robert Constable that made the present campus a thing of beauty.

And today, in 1976, each of the more than five hundred full-time employees is a part of this long procession of the faithful. Their work, too, in many instances, will be recognized only by God. Many of them are members of the Institute's Diamond Pin Club which acknowledges twenty-five years of service. Of course years of employment do not automatically insure quality of work. But MBI employees realize that their work is more than a job; it is a commitment to service. Each year Moody graduates are asked to give as serious consideration to employment at the Institute as they do to God's call to a mission field.

For after all, the typist filling an order for Moody Press books is a part of God's strategy for reaching men and women with the Gospel. So is the faculty member teaching his classes, and the dean helping to lift a student burden. It is no less true of the registrar overseeing records, the cooks preparing meals, the security guard protecting life and property, or the janitor cleaning floors. Each is responding to the command, "Let your light so shine before men, that they may see your good works, and glorify your Father which is in heaven" (Matthew 5:16) — the treasure in earthen vessels, reflecting to God's glory.

To each past and present employee comes heartfelt thanks from the members of the board of trustees:

E. Richard Tallmadge, James N. Mathias, Gerrit Wit, James H. Barnes, Robert G. Dunlop, Elner A. Edman, John Elsen, Robert E. Foltz, Richard E. Gildner, Edgar A. Harrell, W. Maxey Jarman, Edward L. Johnson, Robert E. Nicholas, Wallace L. Pepin, and George Sweeting.

And from the officers of the Institute:

George Sweeting, President; Donald E. Hescott, Executive Vice-president and General Manager; Alfred Martin, Vice-President and Dean of Education; E. Brandt Gustavson, Vice-President and Administrator of Development; Richard E. Sackett, Vice-President and Manager of Investments; Lowell L. Kline, Vice-President and Treasurer; Marvin E. Beckman, Vice-President and General Counsel; and Donald E. Campbell, Vice-president of Administrative Services.

But the crowning reward for any service is not the praise of men. It is to hear God's "Well done, thou good and faithful servant . . . enter thou into the joy of thy lord" (Matthew 25:21) .

Notes

1. Gene Getz, *The Story of Moody Bible Institute* (Chicago: Moody, 1969), p. 36.
2. William Moody, *The Life of Dwight L. Moody* (New York: Revell, 1900), p. 344.
3. Richard Ellsworth Day, *Breakfast Table Autocrat* (Chicago: Moody, 1946), pp. 175-76.
4. Ibid., 306-7.
5. William M. Runyan, *Dr. Gray at Moody Bible Institute* (New York: Oxford U., 1935), p. 14.
6. Ibid., p. 136.
7. Ibid., p. 43.
8. Wilbur Smith, *A Watchman on the Wall* (Grand Rapids: Eerdmans, 1951), pp. 112-13.
9. Ibid., pp. 128-29.
10. Warren Wiersbe, *William Culbertson: A Man of God* (Chicago: Moody, 1974), p. 67.
11. Ibid., p. 88.
12. Getz, p. 251.
13. Wiersbe, p. 105.
14. Ibid., p. 160.